Knight Moves

THE K J KNIGHT STORY SECOND EDITION

K J KNIGHT

Order this book online at www.trafford.com
or email orders@trafford.com

Most Trafford titles are also available at major online book retailers.

Print information available on the last page.

ISBN: 978-1-6987-0007-6 (sc)
ISBN: 978-1-6987-0010-6 (e)

Trafford rev. 03/10/2020

www.trafford.com

North America & international
toll-free: 1 888 232 4444 (USA & Canada)
fax: 812 355 4082

This book is dedicated to the memory of my dear friend and bandmate, Sonny Cingolani, who passed away on November 25, 2019 at the age of 72.

"Who speaks of victory? To endure is all."
—Rainer Maria Rilke—

CONTENTS

Acknowledgements

A special loving thank-you to my wife, Connie, for supporting me in writing this book and balancing my life.

Thanks to my children, Kenny, Michael, and Starr. I am so proud of all of you.

Much thanks to my mother, Eleanor Mills, for her unconditional love.

I'm forever grateful to Maurie Jones for her editorial assistance, keen insight, and ongoing support in bringing my stories to life.

In addition, my deep gratitude goes to Ted Nugent. Thanks for giving me my fifteen minutes of fame.

INTRODUCTION

May 9, 1970, Montreal Forum—the place was packed; more than 17,000 strong. To wind up a blistering set of high energy Detroit-style rock and roll, Ted Nugent, clad in a skintight white fringed jumpsuit and a studded leather belt, leaned back against his towering stack of Fender amps and let loose on his Byrdland guitar with a series of sustained high-pitched screams. Upon that primal wail, I catapulted from behind my drum set and dropped onto the stage next to Ted. Crouching on one knee, I grabbed his microphone stand and held the mic six inches from his face as he roared:

"Now, our ears are one! Our ears are married! May they melt together to the ends of the eeeeeaaaaarth!"

Following this choreographed moment, I rushed back to my drums while Nugent began his search for the ultimate note. When he found that show-stopping note, its lengthy, ear-piercing shriek was like that of a siren sounding a warning signal. And, in accompaniment, that siren formed a wall of decibels speeding at the audience with the force of a 300 mph F5 Tornado.

As we thrashed through our finale, I grabbed my hi-hat stand with cymbals attached and started twirling it over my head like a baton. In my frenzy, I got too close to our bass player, Greg Arama, and caught him square in the forehead with the spinning hi-hat stand, cymbals and all. Blood was streaming down Greg's face; undeterred, he kept right on playing. Still driven by the intensity of the moment, I hurled my hi-hat out into the crowd, cymbals rotating wildly like flaming sabers. Then I flipped my crash cymbal and stand upside down, stomped onto the inverted cymbal, and, gripping the stand with both hands, began bouncing around on stage as if mounted on a pogo stick.

While my mania was raging, Ted shoved his feedbacking guitar up against his amps and took a running head-first dive off the ten-foot high stage, disappearing into a blurry universe of French-Canadian stoners. Unrestrainable now and with ferocious intensity, I grabbed my crash cymbal and, in a Frisbee-like motion, flung it into the crowd. Just as I was rearing back to begin my next maneuver, the house lights abruptly came on. Unable to see due to the intensity of the glare, I blindly and mightily spear-chucked my cymbal-stand into the dark abyss that was the audience.

Engulfed in the madness and without warning, Dave Leggett, a backstage roadie, decided to get into the act. He bolted onto the stage and seized my entire bass drum apparatus, complete with mounted toms attached and sharp metal spurs, and launched it into the crowd. Almost as if part of the show, drum parts hailed down on several fans like tornadic debris as they cowered against the in-coming.

Moments later, at the sight of Greg Arama and our keyboard player, Andy Solomon dashing backstage, I realized that all who remained onstage was me. Ascending a barren drum riser, I stood tall and raised my arms—a victorious warlord.

Our part of the concert had now come to an end, and as I was making my way backstage, I passed by the

Grand Funk Railroad who were scheduled to go on next and who had been watching our show from the side of the stage. I looked their way, smiled, and offered up a sarcastic, "Good luck," as it was obvious that our no-holds-barred performance would be a tough act to follow.

When I got to the dressing room, our road manager, Phil Nicholson, informed me that several people in the audience had been injured by flying parts of my drum set and as a precaution, three of them had been taken by ambulance to a nearby hospital for treatment. Phil mentioned too that the promoter of the concert was holding back our payment because he was concerned that the injured concertgoers might file lawsuits against him. He added that Arama was also headed to the hospital as it appeared he needed stiches for the nasty gash on his face. I felt terrible about what had happened to Greg and decided I should go with him.

A day earlier, before leaving for Montreal, Nugent had pulled me aside and told me that in appreciation for my dedication and hard work, he'd ordered me a new set of custom-made mahogany Ludwig drums through Al Nalli Music in Ann Arbor, Michigan. They were due to arrive within the next few days. Ted and I decided then, that at the end of our performance at the Forum the next night, we'd add a little excitement to the show. The plan was that I'd dismantle my soon-to-be-replaced set of drums and toss the pieces into the crowd as souvenirs, à la Keith Moon. It never occurred to us that anyone would get hurt.

While waiting in the emergency room for Arama to get stitched up, a kid with his head wrapped in a gauze bandage looked my way and began to walk over. It turns out he'd been at the concert and recognized me. Holding a bent cymbal stand in one hand and felt pen in the other, he beamed and said, "That was the greatest show I've ever seen!" and then asked me to autograph the stand. Despite the fact that a few who attended our performance suffered some bumps, cuts, and bruises that night, no one was seriously injured and no lawsuits were filed.

Three months later, we returned to Montreal to do another show and learned that rock fans who had attended our Forum concert were still abuzz about our onstage antics. Following a sound check for that evening's performance, the backers of the event presented the band with a large concert poster. There, under the name "The Amboy Dukes," was a picture of me onstage at the Forum with a cymbal stand clenched in my fist. I must say that I was totally blown away by this gesture of recognition and felt extremely honored.

Chapter One: Getting Started

$\mathscr{I}$ was fourteen years old when I saw The Beatles' 1964 debut performance on The Ed Sullivan Show. From that moment on, I knew I wanted to play in a band. My family was upper middle class and lived in Westland, Michigan, a suburb of Detroit. My father, Donald William Mills, was a professional drummer and, while in the service during WWII, played in the Navy band wherever he was stationed. He could read music and was extremely adept at playing rudiments and Latin beats. He was also good with brushes. He owned two sets of Ludwig drums, one of which was kept in our basement. I asked my dad on many occasions if he would teach me how to play and each time, he pretty much blew me off. But I was determined, so after months of badgering him, one day he finally broke down and said yes. He bought me a rubber practice pad and a heavy pair of drumsticks and attempted to teach me some fundamentals. I tried to follow along but couldn't comprehend his instructions. After only ten minutes he lost his patience and gave up on me.

So, I taught myself how to play. The first thing I did was throw that damn practice pad in the trash. Then I sat down at my dad's drum set and banged along to the music on my portable transistor radio until, eventually, I learned to play by ear. Once I got the hang of it and was able to master a few basic beats and a fill or two, I got together with some other teenaged musician-wannabes in the area and formed a band.

My first group was The Stingers, consisting of me and three others: neighborhood friends, Lee Huntley and Al Zsenyuk, and fellow classmate, Jack McCarthy. Lee sang lead vocals and played guitar (some lead but mainly rhythm), Al played bass and sang backup vocals, and Jack, who answered to the nickname "Toad," was on lead guitar. We mostly played Beatles songs and were reputed to look "adorable" in our matching blue velour sweaters. We played a couple of after-school functions at my old alma mater, Whittier Junior High School, and a few Friday afternoon parties at campus frat houses at the University of Michigan. Since none of us was old enough to have a driver's license, our mothers had to drive us to and from every gig.

My mother, Eleanor Simmers Mills, was an attractive woman who bore a striking resemblance to Jacqueline Kennedy. Shy and reserved, she was a stay-at-home mom with no formal employment skills, although she did possess a natural talent for sewing and knitting. I recall she was very supportive of me and my endeavors, but I really don't remember much else about her from my childhood—during that time, my dad was the center of my world.

I was an only child. My father was an only child, and his father was an only child. Dad was a portly man, who was highly sensitive about his oversized physique—so much so that in an attempt to deflect disparaging remarks, he was quick to make fun of himself before anyone else could take a shot at him. He often referred to himself as "L. A." (Lard Ass) or "Willie the Whale."

He was self-employed and worked from home, having made a niche for himself in the collection business by conducting asset investigations and skiptrace investigations for insurance companies and law firms. He was also the leader of a small dance band that played on weekends at weddings, parties, and local nightclubs. His group was the Don Mills Trio and featured his friend, Joe Oddo, on stand-up bass and lead vocals. In the early sixties they cut a 45-rpm demo record on the Viscount label. The A-side was an original entitled "Sick, Sick, Sick, Cha, Cha, Cha," and the flip-side was their cover of the old standard "Chicago."

My old man had more than his share of faults, among them being a con-artist and compulsive gambler. He would bet on most anything because he loved the action. To beat the odds, he had an "edge"—cheating. Sparing no one, he'd have his uncles, Jimmy, Orville, and Reds, over for Friday night poker parties, scamming them by playing with marked decks of cards. When I turned twelve, he let me in on the action. Together, my old man and I swindled the relatives out of hundreds of dollars. You could say that it was one of our first bonding experiences.

We lived near the Hawthorne Valley Golf Course and Bowling Alley, and Dad liked to go there to bowl for money; I'm talking big money, a hundred dollars a game. He'd had a twenty-pound ball specially made for him—the legal weight limit was, and still is, sixteen pounds. Sometimes he'd team with an accomplice who would stand at the back of the alley to the side, unseen behind the pins, black hanger in hand. At the exact moment that my dad's ball would connect with the head pin, the accomplice would use the end of the hanger to nudge the top of the seven or ten pin causing it to tip over, greatly increasing my father's chances of getting a strike. Dad bowled with some pretty shady characters, and if any of them had ever caught him running this con, they surely would have exacted their pound of flesh. Occasionally, my father took me with him to the lanes and let me bowl for money against his gambling cronies. I had about a 145 average, and he would get his friends to spot me 50 pins and have me bowl them for twenty-five bucks a game.

My dad's need to win crept into my childhood activities. Between the ages of nine and thirteen, I played little league baseball. For a few seasons my dad coached my teams. During one of those seasons, our team, the Nankin Mills Yankees, went 18-0, winning us the league championship. Years later I learned from my mother that my father was so obsessed with winning every one of those games, he'd gone as far as to pay off umpires for favorable calls and bribe coaches into throwing games so that our perfect record remained intact. Dear old Dad was some piece of work!

My old man loved playing the ponies and spent a lot of time at the Detroit Race Course (DRC). Many people have pleasant memories of the first time their mom or dad took them to a professional ball game, but for me, my fondest memory is the first time my dad took me to the track. It was a very bright, sunny day and I was thirteen years old. As my father and I sat high up in the grandstand amid a collection of racetrack oddballs, I remember being giddy with anticipation and dizzy from the scent of cherry pipe tobacco wafting in the air. I was fascinated by the speed and sound of the thoroughbreds thundering down the track, mounted by miniature men wearing colorful silks. It was a thing of beauty.

For the last race on the card, my dad let me pick a horse and placed a two-dollar bet to win. I chose Harmony Swing; his odds were 99-1. With my own action on the race, I watched with extra excitement as the horses were loaded in the gate. At the ring of the bell, the gate flew open and the track announcer shouted, "They're off!" It was a close race from the beginning and down the stretch, Harmony Swing and another horse were neck and neck. It was a photo finish! All eyes were glued on the tote board waiting on the results and after what seemed an eternity; they finally appeared, flashing on the tote. Harmony Swing's number was posted second. In disgust, my dad ripped my ticket in two and threw the pieces on the ground. But as we got up to leave, a guy who'd been sitting next to us yelled out that the flashing numbers indicated that the race had been declared a "dead heat," meaning that Harmony Swing had tied for first place…and my father had just destroyed a winning ticket! Dad rushed to pick up the torn ticket pieces, and we immediately went to the Track Information Desk where a kindly teller Scotch-taped the ticket back together and permitted my dad to cash it. It paid one hundred dollars; he split the winnings with me. From that moment on, I was hooked.

My dad wanted the best of everything, both for himself and our family. His hard work and hustle made it possible for us to enjoy a very comfortable living. We owned a nice brick ranch-style house in a new suburb and were the first family on our block to have a built-in swimming pool. Yet, what I loved most about our house was the basement. Down there, my father had installed a wooden bandstand which was supporting a set of drums, a stand-up piano, a trumpet, a trombone, and a stand-up bass. Our basement contained everything you'd want in a popular watering hole: a stocked bar, pool table, arcade bowling machine, pinball machine, and nickel slot machine. We were a close and happy family, and my father referred to us as "The Three Musketeers." He'd often proudly proclaim, "We're Mills and we're better than other people!"

In 1965, my father and a business partner purchased a teen nightclub on the corner of Middlebelt Road and West Warren Avenue in Garden City, only about three or four miles away from where we lived in Westland. Originally known as The Chatterbox, they ended up changing the name to the Club Shangri-La. It was a small joint with a capacity of two hundred, and it hosted local bands on the weekends. Dad worked the door collecting cover charges, and, true to his nature, pocketed as much money from behind his partner's back as he could get away with. A cutup who cracked a lot of jokes, he was well-liked by many of the regulars.

When I was fifteen, my dad had me working at the club as a janitor. This was where I met Tomo (Ronald Chester Tomaszewski), who worked there as a bartender. Tomo and I were both greasers, evidenced by the way we dressed: black leather jackets, Italian knit shirts, sharkskin pants, and wingtip shoes—black socks only. We hit it off right away. After learning he played saxophone, I left The Stingers behind, and Tomo and I formed a soul band, Tomo and The Toronados. We ordered ourselves matching blue parkas with our band name printed on the back in white letters.

One evening I proudly showed up at The Club Shangri-La sporting my new Tomo and The Toronados parka for the first time. Wearing it while doing the mashed potato on the small and crowded dance floor, I suddenly felt something warm and wet ooze down my back. In a nano-second I realized that some drunken moron had just puked on me! I was humiliated, and the smell was making me feel sick to my stomach. Though my parka was a disaster, I guess I should consider myself lucky since I didn't blow chunks on the cute chick in the black hose who'd been dancing in front of me. But man, if that nimrod didn't like my parka, he could've just said so.

My father booked the entertainment at The Club Shangri-La and found many talented bands to perform there. Among the best were Rusty Day and The Midnighters, featuring lead vocalist, drummer, and blues harpist Russell Davidson (aka Rusty Day); Billie Lee and The Rivieras, featuring lead vocalist William Levise, Jr. (aka Billie lee and Mitch Ryder); The Derringers, with lead vocalist and guitarist Rick Umberzack, drummer Al Gordon and bassist Larry Dye; an all-girl band called The Pleasure Seekers (who later morphed into Cradle), featuring lead vocalist and bassist Suzi Quatro; and another all-girl band called The Debutantes, featuring lead vocalist and guitarist Jan McClellan. My dad became friendly with many of these musicians, and before long he'd formed his own management company and booking agency. The first group he signed was The Derringers and shortly thereafter, The Debutantes. He also informally promoted a local late-night TV horror show host, Sid Noel (aka Morgus the Magnificent), booking personal appearances and arranging for him to cut a couple of novelty songs at a recording studio with backup by The Derringers.

My old man was becoming more and more involved—you might say obsessed—with developing Jan McClellan's career. Drawing on his strong musical background, he shaped her group, The Debutantes, into a highly-polished, professional show band. Dedicated to the band, he worked the phones, successfully booking them at the best venues. When it came to Jan and her band, he spared no expense, shelling out obscene amounts of cash to fund their performing costs, including purchasing a VW van, stage costumes, band equipment, and recording time and demos at Detroit's Motown Recording Studios.

One day, out of the blue, my father dropped a bombshell on my mother and me. He was having an affair with Jan; she was sixteen years old at the time. He said they had fallen for each other, and he wanted my mother to agree to a divorce so he could marry Jan. Clearly, his propensity for cheating had led him from the world of gaming into the world of love and loyalty. At that moment my life changed. My mother was devastated and heartbroken; I was confused and ashamed. In a matter of seconds, all the respect and admiration I'd had for my father transformed into resentment and anger. News of the scandal spread and soon everyone knew that thirty-six-year-old Don Mills was intimately involved with a minor. My unfaithful father's infatuation with a teenage gold-digger tore my happy home apart and turned my world upside-down.

Chapter Two: Early Knightriders

*T*hat same year, Tomo and I merged with two members of The Deltons: guitarist Garry "Red Pie" Reese (Garry got his nickname because he loved cherry pie) and bassist Mike Opolski. A short time later we took on a soul singer named Rodney Robinson (aka Rodney Knight) and changed the name of our band to Rodney Knight and The Knightfighters. As singers go, Rodney wasn't half bad, but he had a tendency to be overbearing and heavy-handed. The rest of us weren't about to put up with that nonsense, so it wasn't long before he was let go and I took the reins as lead vocalist and leader of the band. For recognition's sake, we wanted to maintain a similar band name, so we changed it from The Knightfighters to The Knightriders. At the same time, I'd decided I needed a stage name. Since my full and proper name is Kenneth Jay Mills, my father suggested I use the initials of my first and middle names with the last name Knight. I thought "K J Knight" sounded damn cool.

We felt we needed to include a keyboard player in the band. My second cousin, Ronnie Reinholtz, played a Farfisa organ and was a tad above mediocre, so we brought him in. Ronnie had white freckled skin, red hair, and was a rather odd-looking guy. He owned a Howdy Doody ventriloquist dummy, which only seemed appropriate, and sometimes he'd bring it with him to gigs. When we let him, he'd carry it on stage and introduce some of our songs with the puppet. In a strange high-pitched voice, he'd say, "Howdy Doody everybody! Here's one by James Brown! I Feel Good!" Before long, people began referring to Ronnie as Howdy. But along with his upbeat weirdness, Ronnie had a dark side. When he was a kid, he tortured his pet hamsters. Once, he bounced a pregnant hamster up and down on his bed in hopes that the babies would be born deformed. He also burned some with an acetylene torch.

A few months after bringing Howdy on, we were able to convince Sonny Holidae (real name Louis Alfred Cingolani) to join The Knightriders. Sonny had played in some popular local bands, including Louie and The Fortunaires and The Sandpipers. He played guitar, sax, flute, and drums, and was a great vocalist, too. Adding Sonny to the band made us a much stronger act. Not long after Sonny joined the group, we got rid of my weird cousin, Howdy, replacing him with accomplished musician, Don "Dondi" Stolt, who played a mean Hammond B3 organ.

The Knightriders were a proud and tight-knit band. We were soul brothers, and looked and dressed the part. Before performances, we'd each spend hours in front of dressing-room mirrors styling our hair with Dep gel and Aquanet hairspray. Once every strand was in place, we'd hit the stage, resplendent in either our matching silver lamé jackets or navy-blue tuxedos. Most of our songs were from the playlists of our favorite deejays, Rockin' Robbie D and Martha Jean the Queen on our favorite radio station, WCHB, "soul radio." We played "(The Story of) Woman, Love And A

Man" by Tony Clarke, "Need Your Lovin'" by Don Gardner and Dee Dee Ford, "Twine Time" by Alvin Cash & The Crawlers, "Everybody Needs Somebody To Love" by Wilson Pickett, "Goin' Back To Miami" by Wayne Cochran & The C. C. Riders, "On The Horizon" by Ben E. King, and "Agent Double-O-Soul" by Edwin Starr.

In 1966, The Knightriders entered the annual Michigan State Fair Battle of the Bands contest. More than a hundred other bands were entered as well, playing every style of music from rock and roll to swing, folk, blues and soul. Damned if we didn't win! This was a huge honor for our band. To mark the achievement, we were presented with an engraved wood and brass plaque. On it was inscribed "Champion Awarded To K J Knight and The Nite Riders." (Our success was widely publicized, and from that time on we were often billed under this incorrect spelling of the band's name.) Over the three-day contest, I made sure to check out all the great attractions at the fair. The one I most enjoyed was the freak show featuring the three-legged man. As you neared the exhibit, a barker could be heard over the loudspeaker saying, "He walks, he talks, and he drives a car." Sadly, the multi-talented three-legged man died later that year.

Winning the Battle of the Bands gained us enough publicity, that my dad soon stepped in and began booking The Knightriders. I was grateful to my father for helping my band but still despised him for destroying our family. My parents' divorce was now final, and for me, these were depressing and difficult times. My mom and dad were constantly putting each other down to me and grilling me for information on one another. I was in the middle of an emotional tug-of-war. The dissolution of my family had damaged me and drastically impacted my values and my behavior. I became a deeply troubled juvenile delinquent.

For my sixteenth birthday, my dad bought me a 442 Oldsmobile, a high-performance vehicle that could lay some serious rubber (I had it for about a year before I totaled it). In the spirit of Detroit's traditional "Devil's Night," which occurs the night before Halloween and involves serious pranks and mischief, I drove around town in my muscle car flinging eggs at vehicles and pedestrians.

One lazy Saturday afternoon during this particular phase of mine, my good pal, Lee Huntley, and I went on a furious egg-throwing rampage. While I piloted my kick-ass silver Olds, Lee road shotgun, lobbing eggs at the windshields of cars passing in the opposite direction. We had already gone through almost three cartons of eggs when we came up on a biker with a passenger on the back. At just the right moment, Lee hurled an egg at the biker, hitting him square in the head. Not more than a few seconds after crowning him, we came to a red light. In my rearview mirror I saw the biker making a sharp U-turn to come after us. We were sitting ducks. I thought we were going to get our asses kicked. But suddenly the biker lost control and wiped out, tossing his passenger onto the road. Furious, he angrily shook his fist at us while helping his passenger get up. When the light turned green, we laughed, gave him the finger, and drove off.

Further down the highway, we came upon a hitchhiker. With our last egg, Lee nailed him in the nuts. It was abso-fucking-lutely hysterical. But we weren't ready to be done with our fun yet. We needed to reload. So, we drove for a couple miles to a Kroger Supermarket for more eggs. While sneaking an arsenal of thin-shelled ammunition into our pockets, I saw out of the corner of my eye, someone lunge at Lee. It was the hitchhiker! In an instant, he had clocked Lee right in the eye. I was so startled that I just froze as if my feet were encased in cement, unable to make any attempt to assist or defend my poor friend. Ashamed, I watched Lee crumble to the floor in a heap. If there's a lesson to be learned from this, I'm not sure what it is.

My father got The Knightriders a series of successive bookings at several bars in the greater Detroit area, and we began playing four, five, and sometimes as many as six nights a week. Because I was not yet of legal age to play in a bar, or to even *be* in one for that matter, my dad, through his many shady connections, managed to get me a high-quality fake ID.

We usually started playing at nine at night and would go as late as one or two in the morning. Most nights after we finished playing, we'd stick around and drink or go get something to eat. I usually didn't get home until the early hours of the morning. All the other guys in the band were older than I was and out of school, but I was only sixteen and just entering tenth grade. Classes started at six-thirty in the morning. I was just too tired to get up in time and eventually, skipping school became a frequent habit.

I'd fallen madly in love with the nightlife and with the fact that I was pulling down more than two bills a week. So, I made a decision. I sat my mother down and told her that I wanted to quit school and pursue a career in music. After talking it over with my father, she and Dad decided to let me do what I wanted. I wasn't sure how I felt about that. On the one hand, I was disturbed that they had given in so easily. I remember thinking that they never would have allowed me to get away with this if they hadn't divorced. On the other hand, I was happy as could be, thankful to be rid of school.

Chapter Three: Criminal Mischief

$\mathcal{I}$t was around this time that I met Jim Dasky who ended up having an enormous impact on my life. Dasky was a streetwise tough guy and a small-time crook. He was a few years older and like a big brother to me. His hangouts were teen nightclubs such as The Club Shangri-la, and later The Pumpkin. He became a fan and friend of The Knightriders and once the word got around that Dasky and I were tight, my peers began treating me with a higher level of respect. He was a half-crazy, half-savage type, and it seemed like almost every weekend he would end up getting into a fight. He feared no one and nothing fazed him.

Dasky liked to break into cigarette machines. Back then, commercial establishments didn't have outdoor security cameras and because of this, any vending machine located outside a business was an easy target. What's more, most vending machines didn't have heavy duty or double locks either. This meant that the only tool Dasky needed to pry open a coin machine was a crowbar. His primary goal was to steal the change, but he also stole the cigarettes and sold the packs at a discounted rate to a group of auto factory workers.

Through him I was schooled in this art and became his apprentice and accomplice.

I soon discovered that I loved to steal, and I loved the adrenaline rush that went with it. After some time learning the tricks of the trade, I set out on my own and burglary became a way of life. During the day I'd shoplift clothes, records, and cologne from department stores, and on nights The Knightriders' weren't performing, I'd go cruising the streets in search of places to rip off. I was particularly fond of "smash-and-grabs" (breaking display windows in retail stores, seizing valuables, and then making quick getaways). Most of the time I acted on my own, though occasionally I'd bring along a couple of friends to act as getaway drivers or lookouts. But the guys who aided and abetted me most often, my "crew," as it were, consisted of two trusted comrades whom I nicknamed "Steal" and "Chimp."

Dondi, The Knightriders' keyboard player, was in need of a Leslie speaker for his Hammond organ and they were quite expensive. So, I took matters into my own hands. I broke into a church and stole one. I'd been casing cathedrals and managed to find one that had the kind of speaker Dondi wanted and most importantly, didn't have an overnight security guard. Late one night, with the aid of a flathead screwdriver, I pried open the front door of this House of God and crept inside. Leslie speakers are heavy, so I'd brought my crew to help lift and carry it out. The job went without a hitch; we were in and out in less than five minutes.

But while inside this grand place of worship, I found that I was mesmerized by the beauty of the church, especially the magnificent stained-glass windows. As I walked up the center aisle toward the altar, I glanced ahead and, startled, saw a Jesus sculpture nailed to a wooden crucifix. It looked as though his eyes were following my every action. I felt that I should be moved and maybe even remorseful for this sacrilegious violation of a church, but I wasn't. In fact, it was business as usual. I didn't feel much of anything.

I'd been stealing mostly for the thrill of it; the loot from my burglaries was of secondary importance. However, by now, my passion for horse betting had intensified, becoming more of a need. Equipped with fake ID, I could get into the racetrack whenever I wanted, building an addiction I guess I have my father to thank for. But betting required money, and the only sure way I knew how to get it, and get it fast, was by stealing it.

Once, and this is hard to admit, I stole an old woman's purse. Early one evening, I had a strong urge to gamble, but I was broke and in need of some quick cash. Somehow, I got it in my head that I was going to steal a purse. I brought a friend along to drive the getaway car, and we went to a small, dimly lit restaurant known to be frequented by senior citizens. My pal parked a block away and kept the motor running while I stood near the entrance and waited for a mark. Finally, I saw an old woman coming out the door with a purse strapped over her shoulder and under her arm. I ran toward her, snatched the purse, and made a beeline for my buddy's car. Astoundingly, this little old lady came chasing after me yelling for help. I dove in the car, and we sped off. For a second we thought we'd gotten away with it. But then we realized several good Samaritans had witnessed the crime and were hopping into their vehicles to chase us. Within minutes we heard the sound of police sirens nearing. In that moment it hit us that if we were caught, we'd be pilloried in the town square for ripping off an old lady.

In an effort to elude our pursuers, we veered into the first neighborhood we came upon and parked in the driveway of a dark, unlit house, where no one appeared to be home. Slamming off the headlights and ignition, we ducked down in our seats and waited motionless and silent, barely breathing. After a few minutes of quiet, we felt it was safe to leave, so my accomplice eased the car out of the driveway. Suddenly, out of nowhere it seemed, a speeding patrol car came to a screeching halt right beside us. We watched in dread as the officer got out of his car and walked toward us motioning for my friend to roll down the window. He shined his flashlight in our faces. My friend, thinking quickly and brilliantly, told the cop we were searching for the robbers who stole the elderly woman's handbag. The officer stared at us for a moment then lowered his flashlight, turned, and sprinted back to his car to resume zooming down the street. To continue the ruse of our innocence, we drove behind him for a while and then turned in a different direction, getting as far away as quickly as we could. Finally in the clear, we pulled off onto the side of the road, and I rifled through the purse. Turns out we'd scored close to eighty bucks, a decent amount, considering our trouble. I flung the purse out the window and into a ditch, and we headed straight for the track.

We made it just minutes before the final race of the night, but there wasn't enough time to form the race so we decided to bet all our ill-gotten gains on the favorite to win. Our horse was in the lead the entire race, but coming down the stretch that nag veered in, hit the rail, and went down. The poor creature injured a leg and had to be destroyed right there on the track. Frustrated, annoyed, and angry, we filed out of the racetrack with all the other losers, disappointed and dead-ass broke.

One night around that time, The Knightriders played at the Northland Mump teen club and later that night, after the club had closed, I came back to break in. This time I got nabbed. A security cop caught me as I was attempting to cut a hole through the canvas-covered structure. I was arrested and hauled off to jail. Later, while being processed at the police station, I had to face the manager of the Mump, Hy Weinstein, who was there to press charges. I felt absolutely humiliated. When my case came up a month or so later, given that I was a juvenile, I was let off easy and only sentenced to two-years' probation. But, true to form, I never bothered to check in with my probation officer. A warrant was issued for my arrest for violating probation. Somehow, I was able to dodge it. For all I know, they're still looking for me!

Chapter Four:
The Infamous Knightriders

My dad took The Knightriders to United Sound Recording Studios to cut a 45-rpm demo record on the Sound Patterns label engineered by Danny Dallas and produced by my father. For the A-side of the record, we covered a Muddy Waters song, "Got My Mojo Workin'," claiming we'd recorded it live at the Upper Deck of the Rooster Tail (which was, of course, a lie). At the end of the recording, screams and applause can be heard as can my dad shouting clearly, "K J KNIGHT!" (This chokes me up every time I hear it.) For the B-side, we recorded an original instrumental entitled "Mental Soul." During the song, Sonny and I recite a few poetic lines of wisdom:

K J: "All the corny tricks you've tried, will not forestall the rising tide" (stolen from Frank Zappa).
Sonny: "The world's a stage for all we know; watch the people for the show."
K J: "I think I'm going to die."
K J: "I'll never be the same again."

Once we had a demo record, my dad was able to get us a spot on Robin Seymour's TV show, Swingin' Time, a program for teens patterned after American Bandstand. The show aired six days a week on CKLW-TV; Windsor, Ontario's channel nine. For our performance, we lip-synched "Mojo." (Afterwards, we were given a tour of the television station and got to see what went on behind the scenes, which, for me, was a thrilling and eye-opening experience.) Performing on that show gave The Knightriders great exposure.

For a short while we had a band van, a green and white VW that had originally been owned by The Debutantes. As soon as we got it, we named it "The Knightmobile" and used black and gold spray paint to scribble "K J Knight and The Knightriders" on both sides of the van. It looked dreadful. Not long after, the engine blew. The Knightmobile was part of a caravan of band vehicles on our way back from a gig in Northern Michigan. About a hundred miles outside Detroit, the piece of shit broke down. We didn't have the money to fix it. So we grabbed our band equipment out of the VW, crammed it into other guys' cars, and abandoned The Knightmobile along the side of the highway.

The Knightriders performed at some interesting and unusual venues. On several occasions, we played in the popular college town of Ann Arbor at the legendary Fifth Dimension, a state-of-the-art teenage nightclub outfitted with a professional sound system, custom-made stage, and avant-garde design. It even had a boutique featuring mod fashions. I probably stole more than a half dozen pairs of pinstriped bell-bottom pants from that shop.

We also played regularly at another teen nightclub called The Pumpkin, located in the Detroit suburb of Wayne. The highlight of playing this venue was the three fine waitresses who worked there, Stevie, Cricket, and Nancy Nye. They were fans of The Knightriders and dated some of the guys in the band.

We actually played a gig at a home for unwed teenage mothers. Why we were ever booked there is beyond me. One of the guys in the band must have owed someone a favor. We set up in a narrow hallway and performed an hour-long set for about a dozen young pregnant chicks seated in folding metal chairs. We closed with a song I sang out front on stage, James Brown's "Please, Please, Please." Imitating the Godfather of Soul's stage routine, I fell to my knees screaming "Please" over and over again. Eventually as planned, our guitarist, Red Pie, placed a cape on my shoulders and guided me offstage. During this bit, I couldn't help but notice that all these girls were screaming their heads off. I still wonder to this day if they were truly moved by my performance or if they were merely mocking me. I have the sinking feeling they were mocking me. Oh, the humility!

Once, we even played a men's gay bar known as the Barbary Coast in downtown Detroit. One of the barmen there told me that a ballad on the jukebox, "The Man I Love," was a favorite of the club's regulars. Sure enough, when that song came on during one of the band's breaks, the dance floor filled with male couples, dancing cheek to cheek and swapping tongue. (I also randomly learned that the clientele referred to a bag of potato chips as a bag of foreskins.) At some point during the evening a very large lesbian dressed in a flannel shirt and work boots entered the bar. Upon seeing her, a large group of the patrons encircled her and began berating her and pelting her with pennies. Why they did this, I haven't a clue.

The first time I had "all the way" sex, I was seventeen. How's that for a segue? Her name was Marilyn (I never knew her last name), a bartender at the Shamrock Lounge in Grand Rapids, about 150 miles west of Detroit. The Knightriders were playing a two-week engagement, and the management provided us lodging in a two-story vacant building across the street from the bar. It was quite a cool set-up. The gig was five sets per night, six nights per week, and we played from nine at night until two in the morning. Then we'd party 'til dawn, sleep all day, and repeat.

Marilyn wore lots of eye makeup and had bleached-blonde hair which she stacked high on her head. I thought she was superfine! We hooked up the first week of the band's gig. Three days later, I discovered I had gonorrhea. At the end of the week I went home so my mother could take me to a doctor for a shot of penicillin and some extra pills for good measure.

The following week on our first night back, we were playing "Goin' Back To Miami" and as a joke, on the chorus I started singing, "Marilyn Gave Me Gonorrhea." The guys in the band thought it was hilarious and were nearly falling over with laughter. Once we finished our set though, a couple of the club's bouncers rushed over to tell us they hadn't found my little ad-lib to be funny at all and were pissed. To make matters worse, we were told that when Marilyn heard my onstage proclamation, she ran out of the bar humiliated and in tears.

Later that evening on a break between sets, the bouncers confronted me. They dragged me outside and slapped me around a bit. Maybe I had it coming, but I wasn't about to take that shit lying down, so the next night I arranged for my man Jim Dasky to come up to the Shamrock Lounge to help me get back at those pricks for fucking with me. Halfway through the evening, Dasky came strutting into the club. I pointed out the bouncers, and as he made his way to where they were standing, I noticed him slip on a pair of brass knuckles. He proceeded to beat the two of them so badly they had to be taken to a hospital for their injuries. The police were called, but by the time they arrived, Dasky was long gone. When the owner of the bar found out what happened, the band was fired on the spot.

One of our favorite places to play and hang out was the Huron Bowl in Pontiac, about 12 miles north and slightly west of the Detroit city limits. It had a popular late-night lounge known for headlining some of the hottest bands in the area including Danny Zella and The Zelltones; The Soul Four, featuring Carl Lagassa on guitar; and Doug Brown and The Omens, featuring a talented young singer and musician named Bob Seger.

This is where I first met Seger and saw him perform. He had quite a set of lungs and delivered a song with great feel and soul. Not long after I met him, he left the Omens and started his own band, Bob Seger and The Last Heard with Dan Honaker on bass and Pep Perine on drums. Later, he added guitarist Carl Lagassa.

As I got to know Bob, I started to really look up to him. On occasion I'd drive up to his folks' house in Ann Arbor, and seated in his living room, listen to him sing and play piano. He had a huge influence on my soulful style of play and even on my fashion choices—I began wearing a Greek fisherman's cap like the one he (and John Lennon) wore.

Seger had heard The Knightriders play at the Huron Bowl a few times and told me he was impressed with our band and felt we had promise. One day, in an incredibly nice gesture, Bob got his manager, Punch Andrews, to agree to let us audition for him to see if he might be interested in representing our group. I was still living with my mom in Westland, so we agreed to hold the tryout in my basement. The night of the audition, Bob and bandmate Carl Lagassa tagged along with Punch Andrews to listen to us play. When they arrived, I introduced them to my mother, and it immediately caught my attention that Punch couldn't seem to take his eyes off her.

It was a nerve-racking audition, as auditions always seem to be. Nevertheless, we did our best, and, in fact, we ended up playing quite well. Before leaving, Seger took me aside and said that he had a song he'd been working on, "Caledonia is a Woman," that he thought would be perfect for my voice. He gave me a sheet of paper with some lyrics written on it and sang me the chorus. Then he suggested I take some time to finish the lyrics and come up with something for a melody.

For some reason, I never got around to working on the song (what the heck was I thinking?!), but some forty years later just for the hell of it, I finished writing the lyrics and came up with a melody, then created a drum track for the piece. Amazingly, in the spring of 2012, my man, Sonny Cingolani and I went into a Central Florida studio and recorded a smokin' version of this possibly lost and forgotten original Bob Seger song.

Punch Andrews never did make an offer to manage The Knightriders. As it turns out, he was more interested in my mother than he was in me or my band. According to my mom, during the audition he wandered upstairs and asked her out on a date. Sometime later I learned they had hooked up at a hotel. Just think—somewhere in Punch's mental

Rolodex of sexual conquests there exist images of my naked mother floating around. Holy Be-Jesus Batman!!!!

Our most memorable gig would have to be what we, the members of The Knightriders, referred to as "The Boat Trip." We were booked for a two-week engagement to perform three shows per day aboard the SS South American. The ship was a Great Lakes Steamboat and made stops in Detroit, Mackinac Island, Sault St Marie, Chicago, and Milwaukee, allowing passengers a few hours to sightsee and shop at each of the ports. My father had booked the gig for us. He had also booked The Debutantes to join us during the second week of the gig.

We boarded the ship in Detroit and were assigned a couple of comfortable cabins. To welcome us aboard, the ship's entertainment director had the kitchen prepare us a plate of specially made finger sandwiches, which was an awfully nice thing to do. But after the sandwiches were delivered, we started a food fight, leaving a mess for the ship's housekeeping department to clean up. So, we were already off to a bad start.

The first passengers to come aboard was a party of a hundred or so rowdy middle-aged men who were intent on three days of pretty much just pigging out, boozing up, and playing poker late into the night. Several card tables were set up for them in a large designated area of the ship.

Sonny and I were drawn to the action and were dying to play poker with these guys, but we had been informed by the entertainment director during our initial indoctrination that gambling with the guests was a totally unacceptable and sackable offense. Even so, we were unable to control ourselves. On the second night of the trip, we pooled all of our cash and sneaked over to a table of five players and one empty seat and asked if Sonny could sit in for a few hands. The lot of them, clearly three sheets to the wind, welcomed him and dealt him in. While Sonny was playing, I stood behind him watching over his shoulder.

The stakes were quite high, and Sonny was pretty much folding every hand. Finally, he got some good cards and went all in on a pot of about three or four hundred dollars. When everyone showed their cards, Sonny, with three aces, had the highest hand. Then suddenly, in view of everyone, one of the players, an obnoxious, cheating bastard who was holding two pairs, plucked a card from another player's hand and slipped it into his own. Looking Sonny right in the eye he said, "My full boat beats your three of a kind," and raked in the pot. Sonny and I were both stunned and outraged, but what could we do? It suddenly dawned on us that all the players were in on this and if we were to object, they might rush us and throw us overboard. Steaming and humiliated, we silently slunk away from the table with our heads down, our proverbial tails between our legs, and our money in that asshole's pocket.

The following day, the ship docked in Chicago and the entire band decided to go and take in the sights and sounds of The Windy City. During our excursion we inadvertently wandered into a rough neighborhood on the southside of town and came face-to-face with a violent-looking street gang. Once they saw us, they yelled and started chasing us down the block. They were closing in when we spotted a city bus stopped at a loading zone boarding passengers. We put on our after-burners and managed to reach the bus just in time, probably saving ourselves from a serious beat-down.

After the card sharps departed the ship, a group of about two hundred high school seniors came aboard for a three-day trip. Upon their arrival, the entertainment director informed us that the students would be participating in a talent show and that our band was required to musically accompany the performers.

Shortly after the show began, two adolescent misfits, one an overweight lass with an accordion and the other a hairy man-child with a face full of pimples (hence, we named them "TITS" and "ZITS"), came lumbering up to the stage. The boy said they were going to perform "Has Anybody Seen My Gal," and wanted me to accompany them on drums. I was mortified at the thought of being on stage playing alongside these freaks. When I told the director that I absolutely would not do it, I was sternly reminded that I was contractually obligated to do so. Fortunately, I was able to talk my bandmate, Tomo, who had some drumming ability, into taking my place. I have to tell you, the three of them, Tits, Zits and Tomo, were so fuckin' bad, they should have been bound and gagged and dumped into Lake Michigan!

On the final day of the high schoolers' trip, the ship docked at Mackinac Island and the students, as well as the staff and crew, got to leave the ship for a few hours to enjoy this popular resort island where motorized vehicles are prohibited and the common means of travel is by foot or bicycle.

Sonny and I picked up two cute high school chicks from the ship and went cycling around the small island with the girls riding on the backs of our rented tandem bicycles. After a mile or so we parked behind some trees and bushes and had a make-out session with the young ladies. After quite a while, we thought to check our watches and were alarmed to see that it was close to the ship's departure time.

We jumped on our bikes and rode as fast as we could to the marina. Halfway there, my bike got a flat, so my girl and I were forced to push it the rest of the way, slowing us down considerably. When we finally reached the dock, the ship was pulling up anchor and just about to leave. With boarded passengers waving and cheering us on, we sent our bicycles crashing into the front of the rental office and just managed to dash aboard the ship in time.

Unfortunately, this little episode was "the squaw that stroked the camel's sack," so to speak, and later that day we were notified that we had been fired. The following morning, the SS South American docked in Detroit. As The Debutantes were boarding the ship, The Knightriders were being escorted off. When my father learned what happened, he was so embarrassed and angry that he vowed never to book my band anywhere ever again, and he remained true to his word. He never did.

Over the next couple of months our bass player, Mike Opolski, began missing band practices and showing up late for gigs. He was gradually becoming more and more unreliable, a result of excessive drinking and girlfriend problems. Although Mike was a very charismatic and identifiable member of the band, it got to the point where we could no longer excuse or tolerate his transgressions, so we made a group decision to fire him. This is a decision that I ended up regretting to this day. We replaced him with a guy named Jeff White, who was a more than adequate bass player. But without Opolski, the bands chemistry, which was such a significant part of our appeal, was never quite the same.

In the year-and-a-half that The Knightriders were together, we'd built quite a reputation and a large, loyal following. We might have gone on to greater things, but in the summer of '67, our guitarist, Garry Reese was drafted into the Armed Services. Because he was such an integral part of our group, irreplaceable, really, we felt we had no choice but to dissolve the band and go our separate ways.

Soon after the breakup of The Knightriders, I started hanging out with Rusty Day quite a bit. We'd first met when his band, Rusty Day and The Midnighters, played at my father's teenage nightclub, The Club Shangri-la. Rusty was an extraordinarily talented musician and entertainer. He played drums and harmonica and was an incredible lead vocalist. He wore dark sunglasses while performing and had an ultra-cool onstage persona. His band was composed of some of the most gifted musicians in and around Detroit, among them, Larry Walton on bass and Todd Lovis on guitar. Rusty was known to be a fierce bandleader, demanding excellence of himself and of the group. As a result of his diligence and tenacity, The Midnighters became an unbelievably tight and well-polished soul band, but like many others of its time, it proved to be short-lived. The band broke up near the end of 1967.

Rusty Day was a stage name. His real name was Russell Edward Davidson. To his closest friends he went by the nickname "Pachuco." He had a tough-guy exterior and a hidden soft side. I recently read some online forums where it was reported that Rusty was an excessively heavy person, weighing over 350 pounds. For the record, that's bullshit. He stood about six feet tall and for all the time I knew him, weighed about 180 pounds. I think some of Detroit's so-called rock and roll historians may have him confused with Bob Hodge, the overweight lead singer for the early seventies rock group, "Catfish."

Rusty lived with his mother and sister in Garden City on Balmoral Street, less than a mile from The Club Shangri-la. I really looked up to him; I thought he was the epitome of badass. He was older than I, and I thought of him as the big brother I'd never had. Though he was extremely business-like with his bands, Rusty was very much into drugs and smoked a lot of weed. Due to his influence, I tried it, liked it, and started smoking a lot of weed, too.

Rusty and I frequented a couple of illegal late-night gambling and drinking spots in downtown Detroit known as "blind pigs." But our favorite place to hang was the Chessmate coffee house on Six Mile and Livernois. The Chessmate was an after-hours club that featured music by folk groups and jazz bands. One night we saw the married duo of Chuck Mitchell and the legendary Joni Mitchell perform there. That was the same night we scored blotter acid from one of the waitresses. I think her first name was Gail, but she was known by her customers as "Hester the Witch."

The main attraction at the Chessmate was Steve Booker, a jazz drummer and percussionist. He was a member of the house band, a versatile free-form jazz quartet that played complex musical pieces with constantly changing time signatures. Steve was famous for his unique and creative marathon drum solos.

Rusty and I got to know Booker and soon he became my good friend and musical mentor. I'll never forget the time he invited me to sit in with his band. I panicked and told him I was afraid I would embarrass myself. He managed to calm me with some words of wisdom: "Every musician has his own story to tell; go up there and tell yours." So, I sat in and played a couple of tunes, and somehow managed to hold my own. Afterwards, I actually felt better about myself. Booker (who later changed his name to "Muruga"), provided me even more wisdom. He said that if you listen, you can hear drum rhythms in things everywhere all over the world. Once, with this in mind, I got hold of a shortwave radio, dropped some acid, and stayed up all night listening to the rhythmic patterns of Morse Code.

Chapter Five: Freak Flags

In the psychedelic year of 1967, I tripped on acid quite a few times. On one of those occasions, I dropped what was called STP, a very strong hallucinogenic that lasted 72 hours or so. I took it on a cold and wintry Saturday afternoon; being aware of its strength, I made sure I had no other plans. Later that day I received a phone call from my good friend, Sonny Cingolani, to say he'd thrown together a band to play at a dance he'd booked for later that evening, but at the last minute, the drummer he'd lined up had a family emergency and couldn't make the gig. Sonny asked me if I could fill in. Even though I was high on acid, I agreed to help a brother out. He was in too much of a hurry to provide anything but the basic details of the gig, so all I got was the time and address.

When I arrived at the dance I was peaking, and all the people there looked odd and misshapen. As the night progressed, things got stranger. Gazing out from the bandstand while playing my drums, it seemed as though those on the dance floor were moving about like zombies with crazy eyes. When the gig ended, I was still as high as a Saturn V rocket. As I was getting ready to leave, it started snowing and blowing really hard outside, beginning to look like the start of a blizzard. To this day I still have vivid flashbacks of driving home that night in the wind-driven snow, windows rolled down and radio blasting.

When I spoke with Sonny a few days later, I admitted that I had played on acid. I told him about my hallucinations, that the guests had looked very strange to me—almost like their faces were melting or something. Sonny laughed and told me that the party had been hosted by a local psychiatric hospital and that the guests were their mentally impaired patients, many of whom had facial deformities as part of their conditions. Turns out I hadn't hallucinated after all.

Over the next several months I started going through some major changes. My political views were altered by the counterculture movement, and I grew my hair long in protest of the war in Vietnam. My taste in music took a one-eighty, and I went from digging James Brown and Wilson Pickett to grooving to Jimi Hendrix and Frank Zappa. My choices in clothing changed too, and I began wearing bell-bottoms and tie-dye t-shirts. I had turned into a hippie, and I loved what I'd become.

Around this time, the music scene in Los Angeles was really jumping, and I'd heard that lots of bands were getting signed to record deals. I decided I needed to head west and check it out for myself. My mom pleaded with me not to go; I was only seventeen at the time. But I was determined and told her there was nothing she could say or do to make me change my mind. Despondent, she stood there and cried as I packed.

I approached my former Stinger bandmates bassist Al Zsenyuk, and (my egg-throwing partner) vocalist and guitarist Lee Huntley, with the idea of forming a three-piece group in the likeness of "Cream" and moving to LA in quest of a recording contract. With no persuading, they agreed to throw in with me. But because they were only sixteen, they knew their parents would never agree to let them go. So, they did what they needed to do: they ran away from home.

On a Friday afternoon, in my newly purchased 1959, big-finned, white Cadillac, I picked up Al and Lee from Franklin High School and rushed them home to pack before their parents returned from work. We loaded all our band equipment and duffles into my car, then, with only about two hundred dollars among the three of us, we set out on our journey to fame. The Caddy was so packed, that poor Lee spent most of the trip crammed in the back seat, lying down on top of an amp. During our trek to Tinseltown we decided to name our band "Come."

We drove nonstop to California and arrived in less than two days in spite of the fact that I got pulled over for speeding three times, the last of which was for going thirty miles over the speed limit in Riverside, California. Each citation required its fine to be paid within 30 days. The thought of paying never crossed my mind.

When we pulled into Hollywood, the vibe was electric. It was the Summer of Love and as we made our way down Sunset Boulevard, I remember that the song, "Time Has Come Today" by The Chambers Brothers, was blaring over the radio. The Sunset Strip was crawling with antiwar-protesting, long-haired flower children. We felt as though we had been dropped into an acid-head convention. I parked my Cadillac behind the famous Whisky a Go Go. Then we briskly walked to the front of the iconic club and stood there with hundreds of other young runaways, waiving our freak flags high.

A little while later, we began to realize we were kind of fucked: after traveling expenses, we barely had any money left, we knew no one, and we had no place to stay. As we walked down the strip and were passing by Gazzarri's nightclub, we met a group of good-hearted hippies. A little older than we were, they had just ventured down from the Haight-Ashbury scene in San Francisco. When they learned of our increasingly worrisome plight, they offered to let us bunk with them for free at a large two-story house they were renting, just off the strip. We thanked them and immediately accepted their offer, astounded by this improbable stroke of good luck.

There were eight in their group, four guys and four girls. They lived together and embraced free love and mind-altering drugs as hippies were known to do. We told them we were a band, and they let us set up our instruments in the living room. On our first night there, our new communal family turned us on to a type of LSD which they referred to as "pink wedges," and the whole house dropped acid together. This was both Lee's and Al's first time doing acid, and knowing this, I stood close watch over them, making sure they maintained in case of a bad trip.

For the next week or so, we spent our days exploring the greater Los Angeles area and our nights expanding our minds. Regrettably, the entire time we were in Hollywood, "Come" only performed once, and that was for the good people who took us in. We were able to hang for about ten days before the last of our money ran out, and we were only able to accomplish that by surviving on a strict diet of cheap "food" such as potato chips, candy bars, and soda pop.

Zsenyuk had had a clear complexion when we left home but in less than two weeks, likely due to our daily intake of sweets and snacks, his chin, cheeks, and brow had been invaded by an army of pimples and blackheads. Later, after the poor guy returned home, his parents had to take him to a dermatologist to try to do something about his newly acquired "face case."

Although Al and Lee had phoned home to let their parents know they were all right, they didn't tell them exactly where we were in California. Needless to say, their folks were distraught that they had left. Based on the gloominess of our circumstance—having no jobs and no money—we realized we had to return home. Before heading back, Al and I sold his gear and my drums to a pawn shop. Then, with foresight and a large portion of pawn money, we took to the streets searching for and soon scoring a kilo of high-grade Colombian Gold. We knew that in the Motor City, marijuana of this quality would sell for three times what we'd paid for it, so our plan was to bring it back and sell it for profit to our friends.

During the drive back to Detroit, "The White Whale," as I called it, broke down on an expressway just outside Dallas. We had nowhere near enough money to fix it so we abandon it on the side of the highway (remember: not the first time I'd done that). We felt we had no alternative but to call home for help. Al walked to a phone booth, called his parents, and was actually able to persuade them to buy plane tickets for all three of us to get home. Then he called a cab to take us, our belongings, and what was left of the band equipment to the airport.

Among our load was an old, battered band briefcase that we'd brought along on the trip, which we'd defaced by plastering it in big letters with the names of a variety of street drugs: "MARIJUANA, HEROIN, ACID, COCAINE." Before our taxi arrived, I took the weed we were smuggling and stuffed it inside the briefcase.

Shamelessly, I hand-carried this pot-filled briefcase advocating the use of illegal substances into the Dallas Airport, through the airport terminal and onto the plane and fortunately, no questions were asked. In a little less than two hours we landed in Detroit, claimed our baggage, and made it out of the airport without incident. I didn't know it at the time, but several years later I learned that in 1967, marijuana possession in the state of Texas was a felony punishable by twenty-years-to-life imprisonment. The day after we got home, I took the kilo of primo pot with me over to Rusty Day's house, and with his help, sold it all in less than an hour.

On a sad note, some years later Lee Huntley had a drug-related nervous breakdown from which he never fully recovered. He was in such a depressive state he tried to end his life by setting himself on fire. Though he survived, his torso was severely burned and forever bore the scars of his failed suicide attempt.

When I first met with Lee after his collapse, he told me that he was constantly hearing the voices of Jesus and the Devil in his head, arguing back and forth. At one point during our conversation, he sat still in silence for the longest time, just staring into space, then out of nowhere he suddenly burst into a resounding chorus of "She Loves You" by The Beatles. Lee passed away in November of 2015. Not a week goes by that I don't think about him. To quote Ellis Boyd "Red" Redding from *The Shawshank Redemption,* "I guess I just miss my friend."

Chapter Six:
The Case of E T Hooley

*S*teve "Muruga" Booker mentioned to me he had heard through his management company about an outstanding progressive rock and blues band based out of Cleveland called The Case of E T Hooley that was looking for a drummer. He said he thought it sounded like a good opportunity for me and that if I was interested, he could have his agent set up an audition. I found the idea of playing with an established band intriguing, but I wasn't thrilled about the prospect of having to relocate to Cleveland. After all, Cleveland was the city people called "The Mistake on the Lake" and "The Biggest Hole above Ground," so it didn't sound like a fun place to be. Yet, after a little deliberation, I decided to take a chance and at least check it out.

When I spoke with Muruga's agent, he told me the band was holding open auditions and were hoping to hire someone as soon as possible. So I took the liberty of bullshitting him a little bit by giving him the thumbs-up and telling him I was set and ready to go. He scheduled me for a tryout in C-Town to be held the following weekend, giving me a little over a week to prepare.

I had only just recently returned from my "trip to the strip" and no longer owned a set of drums or a set of wheels. A little desperate, I called my dad and asked for his help. He said he had an old, beat up, second-hand set of drums that I could have if I wanted. He also said that The Debutantes had an engagement in the nearby city of Akron on the same weekend as my audition, and that they could drop me off in Cleveland on the way to their gig. So now, thanks to Dad, my immediate problems were solved.

When we reached "The Dreary Erie," I was dropped off at the designated meeting place on the corner of Euclid Avenue and some other busy city street. As Dad and the Debs were pulling away, I waved good-bye, then looked up at the overcast skies and asked myself, "What the fuck am I doing here?"

Soon someone from the band (I can't recall who) picked me up, and we drove to a house in a residential neighborhood where I met the rest of the guys in the band. At the time, The Case of E T Hooley consisted of Richard Shack on lead guitar, Dale Peters on bass, and Chip Fitzgerald, who played rhythm guitar and sang lead vocals. I introduced myself to them as Kenny Mills. Looking back, this was the only time in my musical career that I chose not to go by my stage name of K J Knight, although I can't seem to remember why.

It turns out the house belonged to Shack's parents, and the band held its rehearsals and auditions in their basement. We started by jamming on some Hendrix and Cream, and I found out quickly that they were each exceptional musicians. After playing together for a while, we took a break and the guys played me a tape of some original songs they'd written. Their material was a cleverly arranged mix of power-pop laced with blues. I was knocked off my feet!

It's an understatement to say my audition didn't go well. I was very nervous and ill-prepared and played poorly by anyone's standards. These cats were so good, that even if I had played my best, I still would have been by far their weakest link. I knew I wasn't worthy, but I decided I really wanted to be in this band.

After we finished jamming, we went out to an all-night diner. I thought I could impress the guys by making them laugh. So, as soon as we walked in the door, I intentionally tripped over my feet and fell flat on my face, then slithered on my stomach across the floor to the counter, pulled myself up onto a stool, and then grabbed the mustard and squirted it all over my head.

They seemed shocked by my Keith-Moonian display, but thankfully they also thought it was hilarious, though a little weird. Leaving the restaurant, they asked me to join their band! To this day I still believe it was my outrageousness that won them over. I gratefully accepted the offer, then caught a flight back to Detroit to get ready for the next chapter in my life.

When I broke the news to my mother, she was thrilled for me and offered to help me in any way she could. I told her I was concerned about my inadequate drum equipment, and, surprisingly, she offered to buy me a new set of drums. The next day, my mom and I went to "The Drum Shop" in downtown Detroit, and she bought me a set of psychedelic red Ludwig drums. It was one of the nicest things she ever did for me.

I moved to Cleveland in the early spring of 1968. By this time I had turned eighteen. Richard Shack arranged for me to stay at his place, so for a while I lived with him and his parents and slept on their living room couch. I spent the better part of each day hanging with Shack, either playing, talking about, or listening to music. It was during this time that I was introduced to the blues. Shack had a great collection of rare records, and he turned me on to such blues legends as Albert Collins, Robert Johnson, and most importantly the Three Kings. Not the ones known as the wise men; the ones known as B. B., Albert, and Freddie.

One day, Shack and I headed to downtown Cleveland in search of records at mom and pop record shops and thrift stores. While sifting through a cardboard box of used records at a Salvation Army store, we came across an old 78 rpm acetate record. It was an awesome home recording of an obscure blues artist whose name I can't recall. But we thought we had a real find, and I think we paid only a quarter for it.

I liked my fellow bandmates. Richard Shack was an all-round good guy; intelligent and articulate with a great sense of humor and infectious laugh. Dale Peters struck me as a rather private person, sensitive and morally refined. He had a passion for vintage British sports cars; I can still picture him tooling around town with the top down in his Austin-Healey convertible. Chip Fitzgerald was an ultra-hip character who had an easygoing, gentle nature. Away from the band, he ran with a gang of Shaker Heights alums.

We practiced quite a bit and played out from time to time, but gigs weren't easy to come by. Shack and Peters were close friends with Jimmy Fox, drummer and founder of the James Gang. On one occasion, our bands joined

KJ Knight

together to organized and put on our own concert at the Painesville Armory. Backstage before the show, I met the members of the James Gang for the first time. In addition to Jimmy Fox, the band consisted of bassist Tom Kriss, and some guitar player they had just recently hired named Joe Walsh (who knew?). The event had a great turn-out and was a huge success.

We desperately wanted a record deal and thought if we could come up with a particularly clever and creative gimmick, we might attract the attention of some record label heads. One of the guys came up with the idea of recording an album with us all under hypnosis. We procured the services of a local hypnotist, Traian Boyer (aka The Great Boyer), and recorded some original songs while under his hypnotic control.

We ran tape while he induced our hypnosis, and once we were supposedly in a trance, he murmured, "When I snap my fingers, you're going to play better than you've ever played before." I'm certain I wasn't hypnotized, but I carried on as if I was, because this was the illusion we were attempting to portray. We recorded three or four songs (two of which, as I recall, were originals called "Paper Rain" and "Horrendous"). Between each song, the hypnotist recited a few lines of poetry or prose. I wonder if somewhere a tape of this trippy recording session still exists.

By playing with and being around this great group of musicians, my drumming skills were steadily improving, and I began to feel like I belonged in the band. I was happy and having the time of my life, but my welcome at the Shack residence was wearing thin. One night, Mrs. Shack caught me jacking off on her couch. Not long after, Richard informed me that I needed to find another place to live.

For a short while, I stayed at a large three-story house somewhere in greater Cleveland with two bohemian artists named Patti and Donna, who were friends of the band. Their house had a gothic look to it and was located away from the street on a hill encircled by bushes and trees. Donna's boyfriend, Rob Ruzga, often dropped by, and the moment he and I were introduced, we instantly clicked. Rob played bass guitar and knew his way around his axe. He was friends with a young, aspiring blues guitarist named Donnie Better, and on a couple of occasions, the three of us got together and jammed. We sounded pretty damn good!

There was always a steady stream of artists, writers, musicians, and pretty girls coming by Patti's and Donna's house to socialize, converse, and sometimes even spend the night. One enchanted evening, a voluptuous girl named Sandy dropped by. I thought she was extremely attractive. We hooked up and had a hot and heavy night of lovemaking that went on until the wee small hours of the morning. I remember that after I performed oral sex on her, she actually thanked me. We eventually fell into a deep sleep and later, when we woke, I felt something wet under the covers. At the same time, I became aware that most of my body was covered in thick brown mucus. I thought to myself, "What did this girl do? Shit on me?" I looked over and saw that she was covered in it, too. Later I learned she had had a baby just the week before, and the brown mucus we were covered in was related to afterbirth. Ewww!!!

With no money and no permanent place to live, it was becoming more and more difficult for me to survive in Cleveland. I thought I might have to leave the band and return home to Detroit. But the band, in a bold move to stay together and try to hit the big time, made a decision to pull up stakes and move to Los Angeles. Our ultimate dream was to snag a record deal, and we hoped our wish would come true in the City of Angels.

When we first arrived in LA, we went in search of an inexpensive house to rent, but we soon learned that anything available in or around the city was priced way over our heads. We expanded our search, and found an affordable two-bedroom furnished rental home in the nearby city of Pasadena.

One night soon after we were settled in, we drove to Hollywood to see what was shakin' and came upon "Thee Experience," a rock club on the Sunset Strip. We heard music playing inside so we decided to check it out. There on stage, laying it down, was the Chicago Transit Authority, and man, they sounded great. We met the club's owner, Marshall Brevitz, and told him who we were and where we were from. He took a liking to us and offered us a booking for the following weekend. Needless to say, we were delirious with excitement.

When next weekend came, we returned to Thee Experience, only this time as the featured opening act. We played an hour-long set of mostly original tunes, and afterward, were approached by blues legend, Slim Harpo. He told us he'd caught our show and liked what he heard. He mentioned that he had some songs he wanted to record and asked if we might be interested in backing him up. We told him we'd be honored and gave him our address in Pasadena. (We would have given him our phone number, but we were too poor to afford a telephone.) None of us really thought we'd ever hear from him again. Surprisingly though, about a month or so later he showed up at our front door.

We practiced with him a couple of times, then went into a Los Angeles recording studio and knocked out three numbers in one session. The songs were "The Hippy Song," "Jody Man" and "Dynamite." Slim seemed to enjoy himself and said he was quite pleased with the way the tunes came out. As it was, we were a few days behind with our house payment, so to compensate us for our services, Slim paid our rent. Regrettably, after the recording session we never saw or heard from him again. In January of 1970, Slim Harpo unexpectedly passed away. The album, *Slim Harpo Knew The Blues*, was released on the Excello Records label soon after his death. It featured some of his biggest hits, and I'm grateful to say, included the three songs we'd recorded with him.

We somehow met a dude named Tom Nieto who promoted rock concerts at the Rose Palace, also known as the Pasadena Rose Palace. (The Rose Palace is a large building used primarily for the construction of floats for the Tournament of Roses Parade held each year on New Year's Day in Pasadena.) We auditioned for Nieto, and he was so impressed, he put our band on an upcoming bill as the opening act for Vanilla Fudge. We played to a full house and to our elation, were called back for an encore.

Gigs were few and far between, so with hardly any money coming in we were barely able to make ends meet. We were utterly frustrated, and it didn't help that we were more or less stuck in the house looking for ways to entertain ourselves. When things got really bleak, I'd try to cheer the guys up with my nuttiness. I'd tie a bed sheet around my neck as a cape, put a pair of underwear over my head for a mask, and turn into "Captain Cookie," flitting around the house like a gay superhero with no apparent superpowers.

One searing hot Friday afternoon, after we'd been in LA for about three months, I took a walk by myself to a nearby public park and came across a group of teenagers (I think they were stoned) skinny-dipping in a fishpond not far from the road. When they saw me, they waved for me to jump in and without hesitation, I stripped down to nothing and joined the party.

We were splashing around and having a grand old time, when suddenly two police officers patrolling the area came over and ordered us out of the water. We were each issued ten-dollar citations for, of all things, polluting the water. As fate would have it, while I was putting my clothes back on, the cops ran my identification and found that I had an outstanding warrant for my arrest in Riverside for the unpaid speeding ticket from a year earlier. Before I could even get my shoes on, I was arrested, handcuffed, and extradited to the Riverside County Jail.

While being booked, I was told that I was allowed one phone call, but since we didn't have a telephone at the house, I waived my right to it. I went in front of a judge and was ordered to pay a fine of one hundred dollars for the unpaid ticket or serve ten days in jail. I had no money for the fine, so I was given a dark-blue jail uniform and put in a cell with eight other inmates.

After the guard on duty locked me up, he looked me up and down through the bars of my jail cell, and then, likely due to the long length of my hair, said in an intentionally loud voice, "Are you a hippie or a whore?" To this day I still don't know why I sarcastically responded, with a gay accent no less, "I'm a whore, motherfucker!" In an instant, a roar of inmate bellowing began reverberating through the jailhouse. A moment or so later, a Latino voice shouted above the din,

"When I get a hold of you, I'm going to fuck you in the ass!" It didn't take long for me to realize that I was in a world of shit.

Somehow, I was able to doze off, but not for long. A well-meaning cellmate woke me to say that word around the prison was that come morning, a gang of inmates planned to attack and rape me in the showers. He warned that no one would try to stop them. I was absolutely terrified, but what could I do? There was no way out. That night, the hours passed too quickly. As dawn broke, and I was waiting to meet my fate, I remember that music was coming from a tiny speaker nailed to a wall—"...my cherie amour, lovely as a summer's day—my cherie amour, distant as the Milky Way..." To this day my asshole puckers every time I hear that fuckin' song!

When the cell doors were unlocked to allow prisoners access to the bathing facility, a jail trustee informed me that showers were optional on the weekends; since it was Saturday I chose to remain in my jail cell. So, while I was safe for the time being, this was only a temporary consolation. I sat there for a long time, frozen with fear, wondering what was going to happen to me. Just when I thought I might snap, a guard came and told me that my fine had been paid, and I was free to go. Thankfully, it turns out my bandmates, concerned as to my whereabouts, had contacted the police and learned of my incarceration. They had come to bail me out... and not a moment too soon, I might add! In doing so, they saved me from having to suffer every straight man's worst nightmare, and for this I am forever in their debt.

It had been six months since The Case of E T Hooley had embarked on our fame-seeking voyage, and although we had tried our best, we were unsuccessful in our attempt to score a record deal and make it to the big time. The band agreed that we'd had enough, so we packed it in and headed back to Cleveland.

In November of '68, we got the opportunity to play on the bill with Buddy Guy at the Grande Ballroom in Detroit. It was great to be back home. The music scene in Michigan was beginning to explode, and new rock bands seemed to be coming out of the woodwork. You could feel the energy and excitement in the air. It was an exhilarating time in Rock City. Many prominent Michigan bands made their mark on the '60s and '70s music scene alongside Mitch Ryder and The Detroit Wheels, MC5, The Stooges, The Amboy Dukes, The Bob Seger System, The Alice Cooper Group, and Grand Funk Railroad. (For a rundown of some of the popular bands of this era you might not have heard of or may have forgotten about, I've provided a list at the end of the book.)

After the gig with Buddy Guy, I stayed on in Detroit for an extra week and met up with my good friend, Rusty Day. He told me he'd joined The Amboy Dukes and that they had recently released an album entitled *Migration*. But he confided in me that he didn't expect to be in the band much longer; friction was building between him and lead guitarist, Ted Nugent, over their opposing attitudes about drugs.

Rusty was a strong supporter of and participant in the use of drugs and was dealing marijuana on the side. Nugent, on the other hand, was vehemently against drugs and had allegedly never used in his life. Their differing views and values had led to an intense dislike for one another.

The Amboy Dukes were performing at a local rock club while I was in town, and Rusty invited me to come to the show as his guest. I was introduced to everyone in the band and rode to the concert with them in their limo. During the drive, Nugent and I got to talking and hit it off quite well. My first impression of him was that he was an upbeat and level-headed guy who appeared to be very serious about his music and career. I had never seen The Amboy Dukes perform and watching the show, I was impressed by how tremendous they sounded, and knocked out by the energy they emitted on stage. I felt that Nugent in particular, delivered a stand-out performance, playing with extraordinary passion and power.

Afterward, I flew back to Cleveland (still didn't have a car), and was once again faced with the problem of having no place to live. For the next month or so, I slept on the couches and floors of friendly female strangers and various fans of the band. One day, I made a call to Rusty Day to check in and see how he was doing. He told me that he had parted ways with The Amboy Dukes and that he and Jon Finly, a rhythm guitar player and former member of The Lourdes, were starting a blues band and were looking for a lead guitar player, bass player, and drummer. Rusty added that he, his girlfriend Marcia, and their newborn son Jocko, had just moved into a large six-bedroom, two-story, secluded house in Farmington Hills, about 30 minutes north of Detroit. He revealed that, since he was making big money dealing drugs, he was hoping to get everyone in the band to move in with them, with him covering their living expenses. Then he asked if I might be interested in moving back to Detroit to join his band. I hated the thought of leaving E T Hooley, but this was an offer I couldn't refuse.

The Case of E T Hooley was a great band, and by playing with them I became a better musician. During the time I was with them, I didn't gamble, and even though I often found myself in financially precarious situations, I never once resorted to crime. My main focus was always on the music. After I left the group, bassist Dale Peters joined the James Gang and guitarist Richard Shack moved back to California and helped form a killer power-pop band called Uncle Tom. I learned many years later that vocalist and guitarist Chip Fitzgerald was able to replace us out-going band members and kept E T Hooley alive.

Chapter Seven: Day and Night

*B*efore leaving Cleveland, I recruited Rob Ruzga and Donnie Better, who I knew would be perfect for Rusty Day's new project. Together we made our way to the Motor City where we joined forces with Rusty and his friend, Jon Finly to form The Day and Night Dealer's Blues Band. For this band only, I changed the spelling of my stage name from "Knight" to "Night."

Rusty's prodigious pad was the perfect band house, and the band was invited to move in. We converted the family room into a rehearsal studio, and everyone in the group, even our newly-acquired sound-tech/roadie, meth-head Norman, had his own bedroom.

Finly was a well-established and successful entrepreneur. Among other things, he had a profitable business manufacturing and selling large and luxurious bean bag pillows. Jon had long red hair to his ass and was known to be popular with the ladies. The guy had looks, skills, and a huge harem of attractive babes. Finly fashioned his bedroom to resemble that of a sultan's, with wall-hung tapestries, Persian rugs, and leopard print pillows. In contrast, my bedroom consisted of a used mattress and a corroded metal tree lamp from the Salvation Army.

Rusty knew the lyrics to hundreds of unique and unusual blues and soul songs, and Donnie, Rob, and I had already perfected several blues numbers and original songs. So, it wasn't long before we had a dynamite set of well-arranged blues and rock material ready to perform. Some of our strongest numbers were "(I Want) Love And Affection (Not The House Of Correction)," by Nathaniel Mayer and "You're Gonna Need Me," by Albert King. We also played an awe-inspiring electric version of "Amazing Grace." I even sang lead on a few songs with Rusty backing me up on drums. My big showstopper was "The Ubangi Stomp" by Warren Smith.

One day Ruzga and I met a group of hot girls, Penny, Shelley, Kathy, and Martha who were friends and lived with their parents in a subdivision not far from the band house. We invited them over to hear us rehearse, and they accepted and followed us back to our place. I guess we must have impressed them because after that, they started coming over almost every day and eventually became band girlfriends. Penny and I paired up and Donnie hooked up with Shelley. Rob shacked up with Kathy, and our roadie, Norman, got together with Martha.

I never heard what became of Penny, but I know that Shelley later dated Ron Asheton, lead guitarist for Iggy Pop and The Stooges. Rob and Kathy got married, only to divorce months later. Good old Norman, however, hit the jackpot! His girl, Martha Smith, went on to pose for *Playboy Magazine* and was *Playboy's* Playmate of the Month for July, 1973. She also had a successful acting career, playing, among many other roles, the part of Babs in the movie *Animal*

House, and Francine on the television show *Scarecrow and Mrs. King.* Shortly after Martha was featured in *Playboy,* I got her number from Shelley and asked her out on a date, but she accused me of only being interested in her because of her newfound celebrity, and told me to drop dead and go to hell. Thank you, Martha my dear. Oh death, where is thy sting?

My encounter with Penny was a one-time event. My go-to girlfriend, whom I'd met through Rusty, was a gorgeous strawberry blonde hippie chick named Brenda. She had a sweet demeanor and nutty sense of humor. Brenda was just my type, and I really liked her a lot. I later learned that during the time I dated her, she was also dating Ted Nugent.

That summer, I received a draft notification stating that I was to report in 30 days to the Michigan local board at the Wayne County Federal Building for induction into the Armed Services. Right there and then I drew a line in the sand. We were in the middle of a war that I believed was wrong and unnecessary, a war I was opposed to from the start. Over and above that, I had a budding musical career I wasn't about to set aside or put on hold. There was absolutely no way I was going to Vietnam. I had less than a month to figure out how to beat the draft. After serious contemplation, I devised an outrageous plan I hoped would work and put it into action.

Two weeks before I was to report, I had Rusty use a needle to poke holes in my arms to make it appear I was an intravenous heroin addict. A week before, I stopped bathing. The day before, I spread baking grease in my hair and all over my body, and then rolled around in dirt to make it cling. In the dark and early hours of Day Zero, I took a dump and wiped my ass with an old pair of underwear and then put them on backwards. I theorized that would look more shocking and disturbing than no underwear at all. I dressed in striped tights, a tie-dye wife beater and a stolen pair of red and green bowling shoes. I looked and smelled like a foul and greasy circus freak.

Around three in the morning I took a hit of acid and then had Rusty drop me off in front of the federal building. I sat slumped over on the curb tripping on LSD. About an hour later, as military officers and federal employees were arriving for duty, they would see what appeared to be a demented madman rocking back and forth on the side of the road. Soon after, other prospective draftees began gathering, and while waiting to be let in, some stood in small groups quietly talking among themselves. But no one dared to approach me as I was, no doubt, one scary sight to behold.

When the Board's doors opened, we were led in and instructed to take a one-hundred-question written exam. I deliberately answered only one question correctly. After my exam was graded, I was taken into a private office to talk to a psychiatrist. While sitting across the desk from him, I kept my head down and made sure to avoid eye contact. He tried to strike up a conversation, but I intentionally remained non-responsive. Then, after a minute or two, when the timing felt right, I abruptly and loudly blurted out, "I want to kill my parents!" For several seconds the doctor was silent. Then he stood and emphatically declared, "Son, I can tell you right now … you're not going into the service."

From there I was placed in a designated holding area with several soon-to-be-sworn-in inductees, where we were ordered to strip down to our skivvies and form a single file line. I couldn't help but notice that all these utterly naïve souls were wearing sparkling clean white briefs. To me they looked like clueless clones being led to slaughter. You can imagine the horror on their faces when they got a load of me standing there among them, coated in grease, and clad in a pair of shit-stained underwear.

While awaiting my turn to provide a urine sample, I happened to see a fellow Whittier Junior High School classmate ahead of me in line. At some point he saw me, and as he stared at the atrocity that was me, I glanced at him and gave a wink. After a moment he returned a knowing nod, signifying that he understood why I looked the way I did and what I was up to. When my turn came to give a specimen, I entered the restroom stall with a paper cup and proceeded to piss all over it, my hands, and the floor. Finished, I stumbled out of the bathroom in a deceptive daze and handed the urine-soaked cup to a squeamish nurse.

Then, I was ushered down a hallway and into an examination room for a physical. Upon entering, I was met with grimaces and groans of disgust from a team of repulsed military physicians. They were so overwhelmed by my dreadful stench and greasy oleaginous appearance that none of them made any move to start the exam. Eventually one of the physicians reluctantly motioned for me to approach his desk where the physical was to take place. When it was time for the hernia check, I was told to pull down my underwear and turn my head and cough. But when the poor man cupped and squeezed my oily testicles, he himself started coughing and gagging and appeared to vomit in his mouth.

After my physical, I was held in a guarded waiting room for hours until the end of the day. Finally, a draft board member approached and informed me that my draft classification had been changed from 1A, Available for Military Service to 1Y, Registrant Qualified for Military

Service Only in Time of War or National Emergency. I was now free to leave. Triumphantly, I marched out the front door of the federal building where I was met on the steps by a fellow draft-evader. He told me that he had managed to finagle a medical deferment and that other than him and me, everyone else who had reported that day had been loaded onto buses and shipped off to boot camp.

Rusty financially supported the band and shopped and paid for all the food in the house, but he was a vegan and never purchased any edible fare on which one could dine—unless, of course, one could stomach raw cabbage and canned soy beans products. Eventually this became intolerable and motivated Ruzga and me to begin stealing food. We would go to supermarkets and stuff steaks down our pants, and then, like victorious hunters with their prey, return home and fire up the backyard barbecue grill (which we had also stolen). Unfortunately, our cherished cookouts could only take place while Rusty was away from the house, as we knew he wouldn't approve.

Rusty had a house rule that the kitchen closed at nine p.m. One night, well past midnight after Rusty and his family had fallen asleep, Ruzga, Better, and I were starving and chose to ignore his rule. We snuck into the kitchen and stealthily searched the cupboards for anything suitable to eat. To our delight, we found a jar of popcorn and a bottle of vegetable oil. Ever so quietly we began cooking the popcorn. But popcorn being what it is, the kernels began popping – loudly. We were so afraid of waking Rusty, that we started fake coughing to try to disguise the noise. Unfortunately, our efforts failed, and the racket not only woke Rusty, it also woke Marcia and the baby. When Rusty realized what we were up to, he charged into the kitchen screaming like an unhinged loon and shoved us out. Then he grabbed the popcorn and dumped it down the garbage disposal. Mercifully, he eventually forgave us.

For months we rehearsed on an almost daily basis. As a result, we were sounding great, but because we never played anywhere, Ruzga and Better were becoming discouraged and depressed. I think it was Finly who finally got us our first gig playing a private party at the renowned forty-seven room Garwood Mansion located on Detroit's lower east side on the shores of the Detroit River. Our audience consisted of Detroit's elite drug dealers, rock musicians, and their groupies. I recall our band was well-received and most of those attending stayed until the very end. That night, I met and became friends with a drug dealer known as Little Neal, who had a reputation for handing out free hits of acid at parties and rock concerts.

A few months later, Rusty arranged for us to perform at a pop festival called "A Day of Peace" which was to be held at Detroit's Olympia Stadium. Included on the bill were The Amboy Dukes, The Stooges, Mitch Ryder, and the MC5. We were thrilled to be playing the festival, but at the last minute, for some reason it got canceled. That really knocked the wind out of our sails.

Ruzga and Better grew ever more frustrated due to the lack of gigs and ultimately threatened to quit if things didn't improve. Rusty told them to do whatever they needed to do; he didn't care one way or the other. Not long thereafter, Ruzga and Better packed up and headed back to Cleveland. Suddenly The Day and Night Dealer's Blues Band was no more. The breakup of the band left me with no choice but to move back in with my mother two years after I'd left.

My father had stopped paying child support and alimony (which he had agreed to pay until my mother remarried) only a few months after their divorce. Without this court-ordered income, my mother eventually fell behind with the mortgage payments and was forced to sell our house to avoid foreclosure. After it sold, she moved into a cheap one-bedroom apartment in the lower economic area of Dearborn Heights, about a twenty-five-minute drive away from downtown Detroit, as this was all she could afford. I hated my father for allowing this to happen, and decided we were no longer on speaking terms.

Chapter Eight: The Big Time and The Amboy Dukes

 ollowing the demise of The Day and Night Dealer's Blues Band, Rusty was soon presented with a great career opportunity. Former Vanilla Fudge band members, drummer Carmine Appice, and bassist Tim Bogert, were forming a new band and looking for a lead vocalist, preferably one who could play harmonica as well. Through their manager, Phil Basile of Breakout Management, they invited Rusty to Long Island for an audition. Legendary guitarist Jeff Beck had already agreed to join the band, but then had been in an automobile accident, sustaining injuries which were going to prevent him from playing for a long while. So, in addition to a singer, Appice and Bogert also had to audition guitar players.

For his audition, Rusty brought along one of the finest guitar players on the east side of Detroit, Terry Kelly, to audition for Beck's vacancy. Rusty had played with Kelly in The Detroit Wheels after Mitch Ryder left in the late '60s. They both passed the Appice/Bogert audition and became band members. However, Kelly was dealing with an ever-growing addiction to heroin and only lasted a few months. Rusty then convinced guitar great Jim McCarty, former member of the original Detroit Wheels and the Buddy Miles Express, to audition. When Carmine, Tim, Rusty and Jim jammed together, the chemistry was electric, and Jim was immediately welcomed into the group. And so Cactus, one of the greatest high energy rock and blues bands of all time, was born.

As for me, I was also presented with a great opportunity after The Day and Night Dealer's Blues Band broke up. My friend and musical guru, Steve "Muruga" Booker, informed me that one of the original members of The Amboy Dukes, drummer Dave Palmer, was leaving the band to accept a position as a recording engineer at Electric Lady Studios (built by Jimi Hendrix and located in New York City's Greenwich Village). Nugent was in the midst of searching for Palmer's replacement, and Muruga had recommended me for the position and given Nugent my number. I thanked my friend and mentor and found that I could barely contain my excitement at the prospect of being part of this great Detroit-based rock band.

Not more than a day later, Nugent called me, and we agreed to meet in the lobby of the Holiday Inn located near the Detroit Metropolitan Airport. Ted didn't have a permanent residence at that time and was living out of a suitcase in various local motels. Nugent and I had met once before through Rusty and had got on well. Already aware of my musical background and resume, he asked me almost immediately into the discussion if I was interested in joining The Amboy Dukes. I told him that I was extremely interested and he said, "Okay, you're in," and it was as simple as that. I didn't even have to audition.

Those of you readers who are musicians might frequently check the Musicians Wanted classified ads in hopes of finding that one special opportunity that could change your life completely—think about this for a minute: I had just been handed membership into The Amboy Dukes—a band which featured Ted Nugent, who, without question, was one of the finest young guitarists in the country; The Amboy Dukes—a band that had a huge fan base and played concerts all across the United States and Canada, and had a record deal with Polydor Records; The Amboy Dukes—a band that employed a professional road crew and owned a spectacular sound system; The Amboy Dukes—a band that provided its musicians ridership in a sleek black Cadillac limousine. And to top it off, I was guaranteed a weekly salary. This was an absolute dream come true.

For the next several days Ted and I were inseparable. We slept nights on the living room floor of my mother's small one-bedroom apartment and spent nearly every waking hour practicing and going over songs on The Amboy Dukes set list, including "Baby Please Don't Go," "Journey To The Center Of The Mind," "Scottish Tea," "Migration," "Prodigal Man," and "Good Natured Emma." Many of these songs had elaborate arrangements, but none more so than "The Inexhaustible Quest For The Cosmic Cabbage," which was a ten-minute piece of avant-garde music recorded and released on the *Marriage On The Rocks/Rock Bottom* album.

Only two weeks after joining The Amboy Dukes, and without having practiced even once with the entire band, I joined them for my first concert at a local high school. I vividly remember that when the band came to my mother's apartment to pick me up in the limo, some of her neighbors saw me getting in. Judging by the looks on their faces, I could tell that they were quite impressed, and as I climbed with swelling pride into the large and luxurious car, I truly felt like a rock star.

About fifteen minutes before the show was to begin, I peeked out the curtains and spotted two excited teenage girls standing close to the stage. I decided to give them a thrill and snuck out from behind the curtains. Then, kneeling from the stage, I gave them each my autograph. But I guess that wasn't cool, because when our booking agent, Dave Leone, head of Diversified Management Agency, noticed what I was doing, he came charging out from behind the stage angrily berating me in front of the two startled fans, shouting something to the effect of, "Who the fuck do you think you are, a superstar? That's not how things are done on this level! You never show yourself to an audience prior to a performance!"

After that embarrassing tongue-lashing, it took me a few moments to compose myself, but by the time we took the stage and began to play, I was fine and not the least bit nervous or upset. We were sailing along and everything was going quite well, that is until we launched into "The Inexhaustible Quest For The Cosmic Cabbage." About three minutes into it, I suddenly realized I didn't have a clue as to where I was in the song, but somehow, I managed to fake my way to the finish. I played my guts out and after the show, Nugent and the others let me know that they were very happy with my performance, which made me feel on top of the world. Things were good! How good? So good that for a week or so I thought I might be God! That's how good!

When I joined The Amboy Dukes, the band consisted of Nugent, bassist Greg Arama, and lead vocalist and keyboardist Andy Solomon. Phil Nicholson was the group's road manager. Arama was a tremendous musician and had a creative mind and sharp wit. Solomon was bright, though quiet and withdrawn, and I never really got to know him very well. I can tell you that he was not one for the after-concert motel room parties and related goings-on, but that probably had a lot to do with the fact that he was married (at least I think he was married). I recall he lived with a lady named Andrea.

Nicholson was my man. I loved me some Phil Nicholson. He had a professional confidence and a wacky sense of humor that I truly appreciated. Phil was a classy guy and dressed quite well, and I was always asking him if I could borrow his clothes to wear during our performances. He wore authentic Nazi pins and medals on his custom-made burgundy leather jacket, which I thought looked cool (back then I never gave any thought as to what those medals represented). I used to go with Phil to the Historical Shop in downtown Detroit where they sold Nazi memorabilia, and I started a collection of my own. Unfortunately for The Amboy Dukes, Phil had a weakness for booze. On many occasions he drank too much and got out of control, causing ugly public scenes which eventually cost him his job with the band.

On January 25, 1970, we took part in a concert at the Grande Ballroom with several other big name, Detroit-based rock bands. It was a benefit to raise funds to help free John Sinclair, one-time manager of the MC5 and leader of the far-left, anti-racist White Panther Party, who had been convicted and sentenced to ten years in prison for giving two joints of marijuana to an undercover narcotics agent. After all these years I can still picture Ted and myself, when our show was over, walking across the vast crowded ballroom dance floor and into a shared dressing room. Sitting there joking and laughing were Mitch Ryder, Bob Seger, and the super-cool Wayne Kramer (guitarist and co-founder of the MC5). These were my musical heroes and it was surreal seeing them all there together at the same time. Seger looked up at Nugent and me and said, "Good job," referring to the performance we'd just given. I can't tell you how much that meant to me. Then Ted introduced me to Mitch Ryder. What a great honor it was to meet the godfather of Detroit rock and roll. He extended his hand and said, "So this is the infamous K J Knight I've heard so much about." To know and be known by these living legends made me feel that I was a full-fledged member of the Detroit Rock Fraternity.

One weeknight, we played a club with a capacity of roughly 300 people in a small town that was located just outside Windsor, Ontario. During our set, I noticed there were no girls in the audience; just a bunch of mullet-wearing redneck guys dressed in plaid lumberjack shirts. At the end of the night, a number of these drunken yahoos got rowdy and started tossing bar stools around the joint.

As Ted and I were headed for the door, about a half a dozen of these losers circled us and started fucking with us. I knew straight away that we were going to have to fight our way out of the place, but I was unsure of how Nugent was going to react. Rusty Day, who hated Ted, had told me that as a teenager growing up in Redford Township, Nugent was said to have had the reputation of being a bit of a mama's boy. With that in mind, I was ready to take on as many of these punks as possible on my own. Just as I was about to make a move, Ted hurtled himself toward the cocky gang of Canucks and went ballistic on them. I stood dumb with astonishment and surprise as I watched him beat the shit out of all these dickwads at the same time. After he put three of them down, the rest quickly scattered. It was then that I realized that the rumors about Nugent couldn't have been further from the truth. Ted was no wimp. In fact, if anything, the exact opposite was true. "The Nuge" was fearless.

The Amboy Dukes performed every weekend and sometimes as many as five times a week. We played at rock clubs, high schools, colleges, armories, theaters, ballrooms, state fairs, arenas, and large outdoor pop festivals. On some occasions, we would be on the road touring for five to six weeks at a time. Then we would return home and play a couple local concerts around Michigan and the greater Detroit area, but soon we'd be right back on the road again. We normally performed a ninety-minute show with always at least one encore. Although this was standard procedure, when the crowds were really behind us, we wouldn't stop until the promoters turned the house lights on. We played out so often, and the musicians in this band were so talented, that in a short time, my playing improved substantially. In fact, we were so booked with gigs, there was rarely time to rehearse. I can only recall one rehearsal with all the band members of this particular lineup present. We had practiced for a couple of hours during a random sound check to learn and arrange "Slidin' On," which was later recorded on the *Survival Of The Fittest* album.

As I came to know Ted and the persona behind his notorious stage image, I found he was a genuinely good and decent person. I learned the "Motor City Madman" was brought up by strict parents who raised him to have an extremely strong set of moral values. Ted loved his family very much and kept in constant contact with them. In the early '60s, Ted's family had moved from the Detroit suburb of Redford Township to Arlington Heights, Illinois. Many times while the band was on tour and the Nugents knew we'd be passing through their neck of the woods, they would put up the entire group (including roadies) for the night. Mrs. Nugent was a very nice lady and was like a second mother to us all.

Nugent didn't smoke, didn't drink booze, and didn't take drugs. He told me that on many occasions his peers had encouraged him to partake, but he always refused. Ted saw first-hand what drugs were doing to others of our generation and found it repulsive. Due to his influence, while I was in the band, the thought of taking drugs never entered my mind.

Ted was the most self-confident person I had ever known. His level of self-assurance was so high, it bordered on arrogance. He had the gift of gab and was a master in the art of self-promotion. Constantly booked for live radio interviews in person or over the phone, it was guaranteed that he would be outlandish, over-the-top, energetic, and entertaining. He was, and still is, a great celebrity airwaves guest.

Nugent played with a powerful level of attitude, energy, and intensity at every show and always seemed to have plenty of fuel left in his tank. Playing along at a frenzied pace, he'd shift into over-drive, shredding even harder and faster. His strength and vitality were inspiring; after performing with Ted for a while, I discovered that my performance level had also intensified a couple of notches. I viewed this newfound ability as a gift that Nugent had mystically bestowed upon me. At times on tour after concerts, Ted and I would sit in at rock clubs, having mapped out some pre-arranged musical movements that featured our abilities. We'd start a jam with a funky, syncopated groove, and from there build to a driving double-time beat, providing Ted the opportunity to dazzle with his tremendous talents.

Nugent was a master showman and was known for his extraordinary live performances. For instance, at the start of our concerts he'd climb to the top of his two-high stack of Fender amplifiers, play a creative sonata of artfully controlled feedback and distortion, then take a flying leap, sticking the landing on stage. Near the end of each show, he'd leave the stage for a moment while the rest of the band vamped on a fast and driving instrumental passage. Descending in a loin-cloth, he'd return by swooping onto stage swinging from a rope tied to the rafters, with a bow and quiver of arrows strapped across his back. At the same time, a roadie (usually Ted's younger brother Johnny) would surreptitiously place a Styrofoam wig head on the top of the amps, squirt it with lighter fluid and set it on fire. Then, in dramatic fashion, Nugent would slowly turn, take aim with his bow and arrow, and shoot the flaming head off the amps. Ted was a great shot; he never missed.

Nugent's over-the-top stunts weren't just limited to his on-stage antics. The band was invited to perform at the Kickapoo Creek Musical Festival in Heyworth, Illinois over the Memorial Day weekend of 1970. The three-day event, inspired by the previous year's Woodstock, featured B.B. King, Canned Heat, Country Joe & the Fish, Delaney & Bonnie, The Paul Butterfield Blues Band, Rick Nielsen and Fuse, New Colony Six, Dan Fogelberg, and REO Speedwagon. The Amboy Dukes were slated to perform on Saturday, May 30th.

Nugent drove us to the site in our sleek black limo. Inside the grounds, we found that scores of festival-goers lying on blankets or inside their tents were blocking the pathway toward the backstage area. Nugent stopped the car and peered at all of us, flashing a sinister smile. Suddenly, he roared, "Ted Shift!" and with a maniacal laugh, took off, weaving the giant vehicle expertly through and around the startled crowd. With debris flying and hippies scrambling to get out of the way, The Motor City Madman with excellent driving skills got us to the backstage without incident.

It was the first outdoor festival I'd ever played at that time, and, with an attendance of about 60,000 fans, it was the largest audience I'd ever played in front of. The Kickapoo Creek Musical Festival and the events that took place behind the scenes is the subject of a documentary film made in 2010 by R.C. Raycraft, titled "The Incident at Kickapoo Creek." Raycraft regularly hosts special screenings of his film at theaters in and around Central Illinois.

During concerts Nugent would often announce to the audience that we were throwing a party after the show and that everybody was invited. He'd actually broadcast the name of our motel and room numbers. When we'd return to the motel after the show, it would be swarming with fine young honeys awaiting our arrival. There were always plenty of willing and able babes to choose from. My friends, those were the days!

After a concert in Little Rock, Arkansas, the notorious rock groupie, "Sweet Connie" Hamzy (immortalized in the Grand Funk Railroad classic, "We're An American Band"), showed up at my motel room and gave me a blowjob. Surprisingly, her technique was really sub-par. Afterward, I felt the need to give her some advice: "Seeing as how you have a reputation for giving head to rock musicians, you should at least learn how to do it well." Connie, pissed, *unsweetly* stormed out of my room.

Many gorgeous girls were friends with the band, but one I particularly recall was a beautiful Puerto Rican hottie who everyone called "Boo." Her proper name was Camelia Ortiz and she was the younger sister of our road manager's wife, Hilda. Boo went on to marry Terry Kath, the highly under-rated guitar player from the band Chicago, who in 1978 accidentally shot and killed himself. (Nine years later, she married Kiefer Sutherland, star of *24* and the Netflix television series, *Designated Survivor.*)

As with most all musicians, looking good and dressing the part were just as important as the quality of their musicianship. Nugent employed Jon Finly's mother, Verna, a master seamstress and fashion designer, to make many of his stage outfits, most notably his embroidered bell bottom jumpsuits. I also retained her services, and she made several stage outfits for me as well, my favorite being an extraordinary red and green Court Jester costume.

Nugent also bought a lot of his clothes at an expensive boutique in New York City called Granny Takes a Trip, an outlet of the original store located in London. They carried the finest in vintage fashions and on more than one occasion, I accompanied Ted to Granny's where I purchased such finery as a red velvet suit coat and pair of multicolor patch snakeskin boots.

When we weren't on the road, Greg Arama stayed with his parents in Redford. Andy Solomon lived with his wife in Ann Arbor and Phil Nicholson and his wife resided in downtown Detroit. I was stuck living with my mom and Nugent still didn't have a permanent residence.

Ted and I decided to get a place together, and we found a two-bedroom apartment on Division Street near the heart of Ann Arbor. Nugent bought a stylish king-size bed and hung Oriental tapestries on the walls of his bedroom. As I had many times before, I slept on a used mattress that I had picked up from a Salvation Army store, and rather than exotic displays of art, I covered my bedroom walls in aluminum foil. Much like the odd couple, Nugent was fussy neat freak, Felix Unger, and I was the slob, Oscar Madison.

While talking with Ted at the kitchen table one day, he dropped the bombshell that a girlfriend of his named Brenda told him she was pregnant with his baby. I told him I knew the Brenda he was speaking of and that I had dated her, too. We compared notes, did the math, and realized that either one of us could be the father of her child. I remember Ted blurting out, "Hell KJ, the kid's probably yours." Brenda eventually gave birth to a girl. Not long after, I learned through Ted that Brenda had named him the father on the birth certificate. We figured she somehow knew it was Ted's, so we took her at her word. But going forward, I often wondered if the child was actually mine. I even talked to my mother about it.

During another of our kitchen table conversations, the subject of the draft came up. I recounted to Ted the crazy way I'd beaten it and in turn asked about his draft status. He said he'd received a selective service student deferment. Years later, in the October 1977 issue of *High Times,* I read an interview that Ted had given to the magazine. In this article, Nugent was asked how he'd avoided the draft. As I was reading his response, it became immediately obvious to me that for the purpose of sensationalism, Ted had cited my draft-dodging antics, with a few embellishments, as having been his own. Since this article, Nugent has been derided by his critics as being a draft-dodger. But now you know that Ted, in his flamboyant manner, had decided on an impulse to use my story. I hope this clears this issue up once and for all!

The Amboy Dukes were extremely popular in Florida and often performed at many high-profile venues throughout the Sunshine State, including Pirates World Amusement Park in Miami and the Sportatorium in Hollywood. We played a show in West Palm Beach put on by a promoter/band manager named Mike Jezowski, and it was at this event that Ted first met Mike's sister, the lovely Sandy Jezowski. She was a brown-eyed, tanned brunette who looked like a petite princess. After the concert, Mike invited all of us to his parents' house, where we met his mother and father, Edith and Chester, and his younger brother, Andy. The Jezowski family owned two bars in the area and was engaged in several other businesses. They became close friends of the band, and a month or so later when we played in West Palm Beach again, instead of motel rooms, we stayed at their home.

Just before the band was leaving Detroit for another tour in South Florida, I happened to run into a girl I knew named Beezy. Sometime back, she had come to one of our Detroit shows and afterward, took me back to her place. She must have been something of a madam because when we arrived, wine and three sexy girls were waiting. Together, she and her hot friends showed me a very good time. When I told Beezy of my upcoming Florida concert dates, she mentioned that she and her girlfriends would be vacationing at a friend's house in Miami for a couple of weeks around the same time. She gave me the address and phone number for where they were staying and said that if I could find a way to come and see them, I wouldn't be disappointed.

About a week into our tour, we played again in West Palm Beach. After the concert I told Mike Jezowski about Beezy and her gal pals and talked him into going with me to Miami that night to hook up with them. I phoned Beezy and told her I was on my way and I was bringing a friend. Before we left, Jezowski filled a big thermos with lemonade and every kind of alcohol he had on hand. Around two in the morning we set out in Jezowski's brand new, olive green Oldsmobile Cutlass; he made me drive. We were guzzling down the booze the whole way, and by the time we made it to the Miami city limits, we were smashed.

Only two blocks from our destination and doing about 45 miles per hour, I attempted a sharp right-hand turn onto a two-lane gravel road. Into the turn, I applied the brakes but they locked up. We skidded for about 25 feet and crashed into a telephone pole, badly damaging the front end of the Cutlass. I remember looking over at Jezowski who was yelling at me, "You wrecked my brand new car!" His head had hit the windshield and was bleeding. My face had hit the steering wheel, and I was bleeding, too. I recall muttering, "I'm sorry man," and moments later, I passed out. We never made it to Beezy's.

When I regained consciousness, I was in a cell at the Miami-Dade Police Station, handcuffed to a stretcher. Sometime later that day, Nugent showed up and got me out of jail. He must have done some fast talking on my behalf, because I was released with only a warning. My memory is a bit foggy on this, but in spite of Ted's views on inebriation, I don't remember him being upset with me over this incident. Luckily, neither Jezowski nor I was badly injured, just a bit shaken up, and fortunately, Jezowski carried enough auto insurance to cover the cost of repairs for his vehicle. In spite of our ill-fated misadventure, he and I remained friends.

In late spring, Greg Arama left The Amboy Dukes to play with Dick Wagner's new band, Ursa Major. Dick Wagner, known to fans and friends as, "The Maestro of Rock," was a guitarist, songwriter, and author best known for his work with Alice Cooper, Lou Reed, and KISS. He also fronted his own Michigan-based bands, The Frost and The Bossmen. On my recommendation, Nugent hired my former Day and Night Dealer's Blues Band bandmate, Rob Ruzga to replace Arama, without ever hearing him play a note. Then, shortly thereafter, Ted changed the name of the band from The Amboy Dukes to Ted Nugent and The Amboy Dukes.

Ruzga pulled up his Cleveland stakes and moved to Ann Arbor. Ted and I had him move in with us, and Ruzga and I shared my bedroom. Yet again, I purchased a cheap used mattress from the good old Salvation Army store, this time for Rob. As word of our address got around, lots of young female fans began showing up at the apartment to visit. Late one night a group of "dress-over-the-head party girls" came by and joined me in my room for a game of strip poker. One of the girls instantly stood out to me from the others. She was a slim, blonde-haired beauty, with ghost-white skin, a sexy deep voice, and wide, piercing eyes. About halfway through the game, I asked the other ladies to leave. Once they were gone, this sexy girl and I finished the game, and then we got it on. Her name was Wendy, and she became my first serious girlfriend. I think we were about a month or so into our relationship before she informed me that her first name was pronounced "Wendy," not "Windy."

K J Knight and The Knightriders
The Pumpkin nightclub, Detroit, 1966
(Top center) K J Knight
(Middle left to right) Mike Opolski, Ronnie
"Howdy" Reinholtz, Garry Reese
(Bottom center) Tomo
(Photo courtesy of Garry Reese)

A rare promotional photo of The Knightriders, 1967
(Top left to right) Tomo, K J Knight, Sonny Cingolani
(Bottom left to right) Jeff White, Don Stolt, Garry Reese
(Personal Collection)

The Case of E T Hooley
Recording studio with Slim Harpo, Los Angeles, California, 1968
(Left to right) Chip Fitzgerald, K J Knight,
Richard Shack, Dale Peters
(Photo courtesy of Richard Shack)

Ted Nugent and The Amboy Dukes
Farmington, Michigan, 1970
(Standing) Ted Nugent
(Seated left to right) K J Knight, Andy Solomon, Rob Ruzga
(©Tom Wright. All Rights Reserved, used by permission)

**The Lavender Hill Mob on a break between sets
Village Lounge, Allen Park, Michigan, 1972**
(Left to right) K J Knight, Sonny Cingolani, Bill Platt, Gary Beam
(Photo courtesy of Gary Beam)

**K J Knight singing onstage
Hollywood Sportatorium, 1977**
(Personal Collection)

Rusty & K J: The original "Blues Brothers"
Hanging out at a party in Longwood, Florida, 1981
(From left to right) Rusty, K J
(Personal Collection)

Dad and Jan
Date unknown
(Personal Collection)

K J's Kids
Altamonte Springs, Florida, 2015
(Left to right) Kenny, Starr, Michael
(Personal Collection)

WRONG striking a pose in the dressing room
Hard Rock Live Orlando, Florida, 2001
(Left to right) K J, Bryan, Dom, Mark, Chad
(©Hard Rock Café International [USA], Inc.)

Treble Damage about to take the stage
Buster's Bistro, Sanford, Florida, 2020
(Left to right) Dan O'Brien, Don Jensen, Yvonne
Belle, K J Knight, Dave Cannella, Steve Ball
(Photo courtesy of Dawn Chiary Ball)

K J and Connie celebrating their 46th wedding anniversary
Seasons 52, Altamonte Springs, Florida, March 2nd, 2020
(Personal collection)

Chapter Nine:
Survival Of The Fittest

*T*he Amboy Dukes had signed a two-album record deal with Polydor Records. *Marriage On The Rocks/Rock Bottom* was the group's first release with this label performed by band members Nugent, Arama, Solomon, and Palmer. In accordance with the terms of Nugent's contract with Polydor, it was time to record the next album. Ted chose to title it *Survival Of The Fittest*. The initial plan was to cut one side in the studio and record one side live, but it was later decided that the entire album would be recorded live. To spare the expense of renting a rehearsal studio, we practiced for the album in the atom-sized living room of our Ann Arbor apartment. Ted had already written five songs for the record: "Survival Of The Fittest," "Rattle My Snake," "Mr. Jones' Hanging Party," "Papa's Will," and "Slidin' On." He planned to include a new extended version of "Prodigal Man," which originally appeared on The Amboy Dukes' *Migration* album released in April, 1968. Although Nugent wrote all the words and music for the new album, Andy, Rob, and I had a big hand in arranging the material.

To show his appreciation, Ted gave each of us partial songwriter's credit for the title track.

Survival Of The Fittest was recorded live at Detroit's Eastown Theater on July 31 and August 1, 1970. The Eastown was a classic, old-time movie theater that had great acoustics and was a fan-favorite venue. Until the sound engineers pressed RECORD, it didn't actually hit me that by performing on this album, fans and fellow musicians would know and remember my name.

When we were all set and ready to start the show, famed stoner emcee, Dave Miller, staggered out and introduced the band: "Ooookaaay, let's welcome The Amboy Dukes!" The curtains opened, the lights lit the stage, and we were off and running and ready to rock. As a calculated tease, Nugent started the show by playing the opening to "Journey To The Center Of The Mind," but after only eight measures he abruptly stopped, blazed out a barrage of feedback, and instead, broke into the beginning of "Survival Of The Fittest." I believe this was Ted's in-your-face way of declaring to his fans that this was a new, evolved Amboy Dukes at the zenith of their talent.

"Rattle My Snake" was arranged to specifically feature my soul-influenced style of play and was easily the funkiest song Nugent had ever released. I sang lead vocals on "Mr. Jones' Hanging Party," which was among the first of the anti-drug songs Ted would write. Perhaps the strongest song on the album was "Papa's Will," a dynamic and powerful piece of music which was the first recording on which Nugent sang lead vocals.

Sound engineer Bryan Dombrowski (who co-engineered the Funkadelics' self-titled 1970 debut album) and his assistant Joe Ford recorded our shows. Afterward, the master tapes were taken to Electric Lady Studios in New York City where Nugent selected the best recording of each song and Dombrowski and former Amboy Dukes drummer, Dave Palmer, did the remixing. Also during post-production, the band went into a Detroit studio to record some vocal overdubs on "Rattle My Snake." Near the end of the song, I was clowning around under a hot mic and blurted out, "OOOOHHHH, stretch marks!" Somehow, that made it onto the album. You could say it's my "I got blisters on me fingers" moment.

Prior to the release of *Survival Of The Fittest*, the band flew to New York City for business with the suits. We met with attorneys from the Madison Avenue law firm of Steingarten, Wedeen & Weiss, whose office managed Nugent's publishing company, G. N. Emma, Inc. There, Andy, Rob, and I each received a $1,000 advance against future royalties for our songwriting contribution on the title track of the album.

During the meeting, we also received the first copies of the finished record. The album cover is a picture of Nugent with a quiver of arrows strapped around his shoulders. The back cover features an image of a photo collage of the Amboy Dukes designed by Andy's mother, Vita Solomon. While the collage is a nice piece of artwork, Ruzga and I aren't in it, since the photo Vita chose was of the previous Amboy Dukes line-up of Nugent, Solomon, Arama, and Palmer. So not only are there no individual photos of either Ruzga or me, the one picture on the album representing the band consists of *former* band members.

While in The Big Apple, we played at the famous Ungano's night club (Miles Davis had played there the night before). I was thrilled to learn that I'd received a favorable review for my drum solo from a music critic who wrote for a local newspaper. We also stopped in Long Island to pay a visit to Phil Basile, owner and operator of talent agency, Breakout Management, who had helped The Amboy Dukes land their record deal with Polydor Records. Phil managed the rock band, Soul Survivors ("Expressway To Your Heart"), as well as the individual members of the now-defunct supergroup, Vanilla Fudge. In fact, when we walked in, Mark Stein (former Vanilla Fudge lead vocalist and keyboardist) was in the rehearsal room with his new band, Boomerang. I got to hang out with the band's drummer, Jim Galluzi, and guitar player, Ricky Ramirez, both great musicians and good guys.

Back home in Detroit, promo shots of the band were taken by professional photographer, Tom Wright at his studio in the nearby city of Farmington. Wright did an exceptional job; the pictures turned out really great. Then, we hit the road to promote the new album, touring extensively. Each time we pulled into a new town, the local FM radio stations would be playing our songs and plugging our shows. And like all musicians who have come before and all who will come after, I can tell you there's nothing cooler than hearing your own music on the radio.

Survival Of The Fittest charted at #129 and sold about 50,000 copies within its first year of release. Even now, when I listen to this record, I feel a great sense of pride in being a part of this real and raw portrayal of Detroit high-energy rock and roll at its finest. In my opinion, *Survival Of The Fittest* is one of the best live albums of its time.

Touring with Ted Nugent and The Amboy Dukes also provided the head-rush of playing concerts with several internationally known groups and artists, among them,

Chuck Berry, B. B. King, Rod Stewart and the Faces, Joe Cocker, Johnny and Edgar Winter, Rush, Black Sabbath, Santana, Canned Heat, Mountain, and the Allman Brothers Band.

Because we were all represented by the same booking agency, DMA, our band also frequently played on the same bill with the Alice Cooper Group, Brownsville Station, and Cradle. I actually preferred hanging out with Alice and his crew who were unique and more energetic and high-spirited than my own bandmates. Alice was a big drinker back then, and his beverage of choice was Budweiser beer. He once told me that he had tried to arrange to have the Budweiser logo displayed on Neal Smith's bass drum head and was quite disheartened when Anheuser Busch wouldn't give him their permission.

For a while, the Alice Cooper Group lived in Pontiac, Michigan, during which time they threw some wild house parties. Ruzga and I once went to one of these outrageous bashes and while we were there, someone let Alice's pet squirrel monkey loose from its cage. It skittered up onto a chandelier and refused to let go. After many unsuccessful attempts to coax it down, the monkey suddenly shrieked and dive-bombed onto the shoulders of a cute little party chick. Then, straddling her head, he attempted to have intercourse with her ear. The poor terrified girl flung the monkey off her head and, screaming in terror, ran through the uproariously laughing party crowd to escape the horror. Now that's what I call entertainment!

The first time we played a concert with Brownsville Station, while backstage with them waiting to go on, their lead singer and guitarist, Cubby Koda, asked me if he could bum a cigarette. For no particular reason I decided to fuck with him and said, "No you loser. Go bother somebody else." Cubby was stunned and really pissed off, threatening to tell Nugent I was an asshole and should be fired. Later, I apologized and we laughed it off, becoming friends.

Cradle, the other DMA band with whom we performed, was composed of the talented Quatro sisters, Nancy, Patti and Suzi. Lead vocalist, Nancy Quatro, was gorgeous; I had a huge crush on her. Suzi Quatro, who played the role of Leather Tuscadero on the hit ABC comedy series, *Happy Days*, moved to England in the early '70s, and through a string of charting hit songs in the U.K. and Australia starting with her 1978 breakthrough, "Stumblin' In," became an international superstar.

During December of our 1970 tour, we had a concert booked in upper northern Michigan. Andy, Rob, and I, along with our road crew, had arrived the night before. Ted was in Arlington Heights, Illinois visiting with his folks and planned to catch an afternoon flight the next day to meet up with us at the venue. On that day, however, a huge storm hit the Midwest, dumping most of Michigan and Illinois with over a foot of snow. Due to the heavy blizzard, all flights out of O'Hare Airport were canceled, leaving Ted stranded in Illinois and unable to make it to the gig. Andy, Rob, and I were backstage in our dressing room when we learned of Ted's situation. The house was jammed packed and we were scheduled to go on in less than an hour. Not wanting to disappoint the fans who had braved the bad weather to attend the concert, we decided to play the show as a trio, without Nugent. We gave it our best shot and, despite the fact that the audience had paid to see Ted Nugent and not just the Amboy Dukes, we were somehow able to make it through the whole set without getting booed off the stage.

Our tour itinerary also included a concert at a Midwestern college where we were on the bill with Cactus, and famed comedian, Robert Klein emceed the show. I was always psyched anytime I got to see Rusty Day and the extraordinary members of Cactus perform. During their show I came out from our dressing room and watched their set from the side of the stage. Robert Klein was standing nearby watching them as well. I happened to notice that while singing and playing harmonica on "Big Mama Boogie," Rusty was bouncing his right leg up and down at a frenetic pace through the whole song. It was comical! I've often wondered if Robert Klein got the idea for his trademark comedy routine, "I Can't Stop My Leg," by observing Rusty at that concert.

In late February of 1971, Andy Solomon parted ways with The Amboy Dukes to pursue a career in commercial songwriting. A year later, Solomon, under the alias Godfrey Daniel, released an album on Atlantic Records entitled *Take A Sad Song*, produced by himself and former Amboy Dukes drummer, Dave Palmer. The album's concept was to take a number of highly regarded rock songs and re-record them in older musical styles. The results are hilarious! Solomon performs all the vocals and plays all instruments except drums, which are played by Dave Palmer. My favorite songs on the album are the doo-wop versions of "Hey Jude" and "Whole Lotta Love."

Andy had been the lead singer on the majority of Nugent's songs, so with him gone, Nugent took on a new vocalist, Dave Gilbert, who had a tremendous voice and was a perfect fit for the band. Soon after Dave joined the group, he had Mrs. Finly make him a white fringe jumpsuit similar to the ones she made for Nugent. The first time Dave wore it on stage, it ripped halfway through the show resulting in a large tear down the rear through which you could see his underwear. Dave looked around at me and then over to Ruzga, not knowing what to do. Ruzga motioned for him to take the jumpsuit off so Dave shed his clothes and began parading around the stage looking absurd in just his tightie-whities, shoes, and socks. I must admit I was embarrassed for him. After a minute or two of this lunacy, while Dave was leaning over the edge of the stage to slap a fan's hand, Ruzga put his foot on Dave's ass and with a smirk, booted him into the crowd.

That spring, we were excited to receive an invitation to play at the Whisky a Go Go in Hollywood, California. The band rarely performed on the West Coast, so this was a pretty big deal. At that time, Nugent was engaged to Sandy Jezowski, Gilbert was living with an exotic beauty named Terry Valdez, and I was seeing Wendy on a regular basis, so the three of us decided to drive there and take the girls along, stopping in Las Vegas on the way. To accommodate all of us comfortably, Nugent leased a full-sized station wagon. Ted drove most of the way and Sandy and Rob sat up front with him. Dave and Terry sat in the middle row and Wendy and I sat in the third row facing backward into the rear cargo area. It was a grueling two-day drive, and on the second day, Wendy and I had gotten so bored at one point, that we adjusted our seat so we could lie down and ended up having a quickie in the cargo area. No one said anything, but I'm pretty sure everyone knew what we were up to.

When we finally rolled into Las Vegas, we checked into the Circus Circus hotel and casino on the strip. Throughout the drive I had been bragging about what an experienced gambler I was and how I was going to break the bank in Vegas. At a blackjack table with about two hundred dollars to my name, I played two hands at a time, losing all my money in less than an hour. I knew I could win it all back if I had more money, so I talked Ruzga into buying my prized pair of multicolor patch snakeskin boots for a hundred bucks. I promptly lost that money, too. Still chasing the dragon, I went through the casino in search of Nugent, hoping I could get an advance on my pay. I eventually found him; he and Sandy were playing nickel slots. Ruzga must have told them what had happened because when they saw me, they burst into laughter, and Ted yelled, "Come on *seven*! K J needs a new pair of shoes!" He really knew how to get under my skin!

The day of the Whisky show, April 21, 1971, we shared the bill with Brownsville Station. It was a blast playing at this historical venue, and we had a great set. After our performance, Ray Manzarek of the Doors came into the dressing room and made a point of telling us how much he had enjoyed our show.

As spring was ending, Ted decided to make more changes in personnel, and within a relatively short period, both Rob Ruzga and Phil Nicholson were fired. Nugent felt that Ruzga's abilities were limited and wanted a bass player more in the mold of Greg Arama. As for Nicholson, Ted could no longer tolerate his ever-increasing open displays of drunkenness.

Upset with Nicholson's dismissal, I gave Nugent notice that I was quitting the band because he'd been fired. In reality, there were other issues bothering me which played a larger part in my decision to leave. Being in a touring band is hard work and a great deal of time is spent on the road. Even so, I was only paid $175 per week which barely covered my living expenses, and I was always broke. Once, to demonstrate my dissatisfaction, I wore a greasy gray jumpsuit on stage at a large concert in Florida. After the show, Nugent asked me why I was dressed that way. I told him that since I only earned the pay of a gas station attendant, I might as well dress the part.

Also, I was ambitious and wanted to be recognized for my talents. And over time, watching Amboy Dukes come and go, I realized that I too, was just as disposable a sideman as the others. The truth was that fans were coming to the concerts to see Ted Nugent, and it didn't really matter who embodied the Amboy Dukes.

After leaving Nugent, I stayed on in Ann Arbor and rented a small studio apartment with Wendy. All we ever did was eat, sleep, and have sex. It was the perfect relationship! Since neither of us cooked, we usually ordered take out. Our favorite place was the Pagoda Chinese Restaurant because we loved their pressed almond chicken. One night, for the fun of it, we shaved off each other's pubic hair. This was a good look for her, but for me…bad news!

Meanwhile, Sonny Cingolani had put together a band he named The Lavender Hill Mob. He called me looking for a drummer, and so I joined his band. Along with Sonny, the band members included bassist Larry Prentiss and guitarist Mike Collins. Interestingly, Prentiss and Collins were former Franklin High School classmates of mine. At some point after I joined the group, Prentiss and Collins were replaced by bassist Gary Beam and keyboardist Bill Platt. This was the first cover band I had been in since The Knightriders, and although being in this group was nowhere near as prestigious and glamorous as being in The Amboy Dukes, I made more money playing local clubs with Sonny than I did touring the country with Nugent.

We regularly played at the Village Lounge in Allen Park, a suburb in the downriver area of Detroit. The club had a small elevated stage and a parquet dance floor surrounded by a decorative three-foot-high wrought iron fence. At some point during each performance, Sonny and I would change places, with me front stage on vocals and Sonny backing me on drums. One time for a laugh, toward the end of the night when the crowd had thinned, I leapt off the stage onto the dance floor, and then, at full-speed, ran and hit the fence gut-first, tumbling head-over-heels into tables and chairs.

When I sang lead, I sometimes substituted dirty words for the actual lyrics. I fondly referred to my profane stylings as "Venereal Material." After our second week at the Village Lounge, the owner, Gus Catalo, lodged a complaint against me with the Detroit Musicians Union (Local 5) for my use of foul language and thereafter, a rider was put in The Lavender Hill Mob's contract specifically stating that I was no longer allowed near a microphone.

Many nights when the Village Lounge was dead and there was no one in the joint except the help, plump old Catalo would sit alone slumped forward at the end of the bar with his face in his hands. Then he'd start pounding his fist on the bar and cry out, "Where are all the people?" which was normally followed by, "I ain't got a pot to piss in," and then, "I need a break." He'd appeal to the band to cut our fee in exchange for our quitting a few hours early. We didn't mind, and on those occasions, Sonny and I would go flying out of the club and head directly to the Hazel Park Raceway in hopes of catching the last couple of races on the card. On other slow nights, when Catalo didn't ask us to leave, we'd spend our breaks playing home run derby with a wiffle ball and bat in the bar's empty parking lot.

Another of our usual venues was an upscale nightclub and lounge in nearby Sterling Heights called Cavi's. One night we opened for the debut of a local comic named Tony Moray. After we brought him on, Sonny and I took a seat in the back of the club to catch his act. For some reason the house was nearly empty that evening. When Tony walked out onstage, it was clear that he was staggering drunk. He told one bad joke after another, each punchline followed by absolute silence. After a few more futile attempts at connecting he paused, and for several moments, just stared down at the floor. Then, shaking his head in frustration, he muttered aloud to himself, "What the hell's the difference?" Sonny and I fell out of our fucking chairs laughing. Finally, he'd landed one.

Later in the evening, when the club was about to close, Tony, who at this point was beyond plastered, asked Sonny and me for a ride home. We felt sort of bad for him, so we decided to give him a lift. As we were pulling away, he mumbled his address and then passed out in the backseat. After finding his house, we dragged him out of the car and left him lying unconscious on his front lawn.

I was with Sonny's group for about ten months when one day early in 1972, Nugent called and, offering a raise, asked me to rejoin his band. After serious consideration I decided to take him up on his offer, and I was once again the drummer for Ted Nugent and The Amboy Dukes.

Chapter Ten: Nuge Redux

This time around, things were quite different. Nugent was now married to Sandy Jezowski and they had settled in the small city of Jackson, 80 miles southwest of Detroit. They lived in a secluded home on a large plot of land. Before the next tour began, I drove over to Ted's place to go over some songs with him. I was greeted at the door by Jeff, one of Nugent's newly acquired Jacksonite stooges. As he led me to the den where Ted was waiting for me, I noticed a deer hoof coat rack in the front hallway. Entering the den, I saw that the walls were trophied with dozens of wildlife mounts, and the floor was overlaid with several animal-skin rugs. An assortment of weapons, including archery equipment, hung on display around the room.

Ted greeted me and, seeing me taking in the room, explained proudly and passionately that he had bagged most of his quarry at wild animal hunting preserves. He told me he felt a sense of duty to nature to make use of every part of the animals he took down. I followed him to a freezer in a utility room where he showed me it was full of venison deer steaks. In my view, his reverence for hunting was over the top; then again, Ted preferred *all* aspects of his life—music, stage, antics—at an ultra-extreme level. Decades later in 2001, his award-winning hunting television show, *Spirit of the Wild*, premiered on the Outdoor Channel and continues to enjoy a wide viewership of both hunting and Nugent devotees.

After rehearsal, Ted took me for a ride around his property in his trusty and beloved Ford Bronco. We stopped at an isolated wooded area and Ted held out his .44 magnum revolver and asked me if I wanted to fire it. I had always pretty much thought of myself as a street person, and for a time I had even carried a concealed switchblade knife, but I'd never held a gun in my life. Guns scared the shit out of me and still do, but I didn't want to look spineless, so I said, "Alright," and took the gun. When I fired that pistol skyward, the shot was deafening, and the kick almost knocked me on my ass. For me it was a frightening experience, and I thought to myself, "Won't be doing *that* again!"

It had only been less than a year since I had last played with Nugent, yet, I was surprised to learn that his current band no longer played any of the songs from the *Survival Of The Fittest* album. They didn't play any of the old standard Amboy Dukes' hits either, not even "Baby Please Don't Go" or "Journey To The Center Of The Mind." The set list consisted of new, yet-to-be-recorded original songs, including "Call Of The Wild," "Sweet Revenge," "Ain't It The Truth," and "No Holds Barred." I was replacing Joe Vitale, who had left the group when he was invited to Colorado to join Barnstorm, a new band being formed by his former Kent State classmate, rock guitar legend Joe Walsh.

Besides Ted and me, the band's lineup included lead vocalist and blues harpist John Angelos and bassist Rob Grange. Angelos modeled himself after Rod Stewart and I mean down to the last detail: raspy pipes, spiked blond hair, and mod attire. He was an outgoing dude and always fun to be around. His girlfriend, Gloria Blondy, was a regular fixture on the Detroit rock and roll concert scene known for the juxtaposition of her friendly demeanor and Gothic appearance. With pale white skin, jet-black hair, and floor-length, skin-tight black gowns, she looked like Morticia from the Addams Family.

Grange was from the city of Flint, 66 miles northwest of Detroit. His style of play was quite similar to that of Greg Arama, and Nugent liked that about him. Grange and I had sharply contrastive personalities. He was soft-spoken and down-to-earth, while I was loud and full of swagger, but after several months on the road together, we got to know each other and developed a bond and friendship.

I got the notion that Angelos and Grange never liked each other very much. Once, the three of us were on our way to an out-of-state performance when the two of them began arguing about something. While I was doing 75 mph on the freeway, the hostility began ratcheting up, becoming violent. The next thing I knew, they were rolling around in a fist fight in the back seat. With my attention distracted by all the commotion, I was afraid we might crash. Luckily, I managed to pull safely off on the road and stayed there until things calmed down.

Now that Ted was married, he stopped partying with groupies after concerts. He was determined to stay true to his morals and remain faithful to his wife. This could not have been easy for him. Everywhere we played, gorgeous women would throw themselves at our feet, especially Ted's. To avoid temptation after concerts, he was now disappearing alone into his motel room.

It wasn't long before I realized that rejoining the band was a mistake. It just wasn't that much fun anymore and the extensive touring was pointless. We had no record to promote, yet we performed around the country, playing almost anywhere they would have us, no matter how small the venue or crowd. The limo was long since gone, so we drove to our appearances in a shitty puke-green station wagon we named "Jerome." Worse than that, the band, although loaded with talent, had poor chemistry and just didn't click. The pay wasn't anything to write home about either. I was only making about $225 a week on which I could barely survive. Unfortunately for me, the thrill was gone.

Wendy and I moved to a new apartment located between Ann Arbor and Ypsilanti. Shortly after we moved in, it was time for another tour, taking me away for about three or four weeks. When I finally got back to our new home, Wendy greeted me with a stunning announcement: she'd started sleeping with someone else and had fallen in love with him. She no longer cared for me and was moving out of our apartment and in with him. I was crushed. I didn't see it coming. After she left me, my emotions bounced around feeling sad, angry and betrayed, but mostly, I was utterly heartbroken. To make this even more devastating, this new guy was said to be deeply involved in heroin.

I tried to get over Wendy by dating other girls, but it didn't help and I remained despondent. I was no longer able to trust women, so I was extremely rude and mean to the ones I hooked up with during my misery. I felt so lost that I allowed my alter ego, the thrill-seeking thief who had been in remission for several years to rear its ugly head; I started stealing again. I was back on Boogie Street. While The Amboy Dukes were between tour dates and I was home alone with nothing better to do, I'd step out into the night and commit petty robberies, and, as I had done so often in the past, break into every outdoor vending machine I could find.

I purchased a 1960 burgundy Ford Ranch Wagon from a former bandmate's father for four hundred bucks and not long after, I decided to use it as a battering ram to break into a camera shop I'd been casing. (I recall that during this heist, I was wearing a pair of custom-made lime green bell-bottom pants that I often wore onstage for Amboy Dukes' concerts.) In the early morning hours of B&E day, I slammed the back end of this sedan into the shop's front window, smashing it to pieces. With a ball-peen hammer and an extra-large pillow case in hand, I bounded out of the car and through the jagged glass opening. Once inside, I used the hammer to shatter the glass display cabinet and placed four or five expensive Nikon and Leicaflex cameras into the pillow case. Then I hurriedly fled the scene. Through friends, I was able to move the haul in about a week or two and turned a pretty penny.

One of the friends who bought a camera contacted me to say he was looking for a hot TV set for a good price. I told him I would see what I could do and later that evening, sometime after midnight, I went out to fulfill his request. I located a television store in the downtown shopping district of Ypsilanti, and when I was sure no one was around, I threw a brick through the store's plate glass window. With the burglar alarm screaming in my ear, I grabbed a

20-inch Magnavox CRT color TV and ran. Lurching down the middle of Michigan Avenue with the weight of the 50-pound TV, I headed for my car which was parked a few blocks away. I could hear the sound of police sirens nearing. I remember thinking to myself, "Oh shit! I'm going to get caught!" Somehow, I was able to pick up my pace even though I had both arms wrapped around the TV and was nearly dropping the damn thing each time it bashed against my running legs. When I finally reached my car, I heaved the massive set into the passenger's seat covered it with a blanket, dove into the driver's seat, and made a successful getaway.

Not long after that little caper, the band went out on a month-long southern tour which included a stop in Montgomery, Alabama. After our concert that evening, I bragged to one of our roadies about how, over many years, I had mastered the technique of breaking into vending machines within seconds. I told him I could prove it if he didn't believe me. Actually, I think he did believe me, but I must have felt like showing off because we got a crowbar out of the band truck and went to the outdoor vending area of the Holiday Inn where we were staying. When the coast seemed clear, I began to pry open a Coke machine. At that very moment, a motel employee walked by and saw what I was up to. Panicked, the roadie and I scurried back to our rooms.

Not more than fifteen minutes later my phone rang. It was Nugent. He said he had received a call from the motel manager who informed him that someone had just tried to break into a vending machine at the motel, and that an employee had witnessed the event. He went on to say that the observer believed that the suspect was a member of The

Amboy Dukes. Ted explained that he had been instructed to assemble all the band and road crew in his room and that the witness, accompanied by police officers, was going to come in and see if he could ID the guilty party. In an effort to head off his anger, I told Nugent I was the one they were looking for. He decided he wouldn't voluntarily give me up to the police, but warned that if the witness identified me, he couldn't prevent my arrest. Under the circumstances, I thought this was a decent gesture on Ted's part.

After everyone had gathered in Nugent's room, the witness and police officers came in. I was immediately identified, arrested, handcuffed and carted off to jail. After being processed, I was taken to a cell and, before they locked me up, a few of the guards threatened to cut off my hair. Fortunately, they didn't. The following morning, Nugent showed up at the police station and bailed me out. So, on the chance that you should read any Ted Nugent interviews in which he talks about bailing out an Amboy Duke for breaking into a Coke machine, you'll know that I'm the asshole he's referring to.

Near the end of summer, I was invited to a wedding reception. Scott Richardson, lead singer of the popular Ann Arbor-based band SRC, and Connie Bedford, his on-and-off girlfriend and mother of his child, were getting married. The guest list consisted of some of Michigan's most celebrated rock stars and best-looking groupies. The party was held at SRC's recording studio, Morgan Sound, and was considered by many as a "must-attend" event. I'd met Scott Richardson years before and, having seen him perform on several occasions, held him in high regard as one of Michigan's top rock entertainers. At the reception, Richardson told me in confidence that he was going to be leaving SRC (which had recently changed their name to Blue Scepter) in the near future. He and his closest bandmate and sidekick, bassist and vocalist Richard Haddad (aka Richard Michaels) were thinking of forming a new band and wanted to know if I'd be interested in joining them. I was intrigued by his plan: with access to unlimited studio time, he was going to make a professional recording of original material as well as unique versions of cover songs and then shop the demo to record labels. I was more than ready for a new challenge, so I told him to count me in.

A few months later, I left Ted Nugent and The Amboy Dukes for a second time and immediately joined forces with Richardson and Michaels. We named our band The Fallen Angels, a very fitting choice.

Chapter Eleven: The Descent of The Fallen Angels

*O*ver the next couple of months, I and my new band, The Fallen Angels, practically lived at Morgan Sound and came up with and recorded twelve solid tracks. Motown session musician, Ray Goodman, laid down guitar parts on a good many of these numbers. On my recommendation, Terry Kelly, the short-time guitarist in Rusty Day's band, Cactus, was brought in to play on a few tracks as well. We covered Lee Rogers' "You're The Cream Of The Crop," with Kelly playing one of the sweetest guitar solos I'd ever heard. Terry Kelly could have been a star. He was utterly amazing and had an engaging personality and exceptional talent. But to his detriment, as a stone-cold junkie, his career never got off the ground. When our demo was finished, Richardson and Michaels officially quit Blue Scepter to assume their new roles as Fallen Angels. Richardson, whose wedding reception I'd attended only months before, had by now separated from his wife and moved with Michaels into a house near the University of Michigan.

On the way home from a late night out, I stopped at a Clock Restaurant on 8 Mile and Southfield and ran into a local concert promoter whom I vaguely knew named Billy B. He asked me if I wanted to come with him to a wild party being held in a room at a nearby motor inn. It sounded like a good time, so I followed him back to the motel. When I walked into the party, an alluring young girl getting up to leave caught my attention. I felt an overpowering physical attraction toward her, so I approached her and said, "Why don't you take off your clothes?" With a gleam in her eye and a naughty smile, she said, "I just put them back on," and then vanished out the door. I was quite taken by her and filed her image away in my memory.

One night about a month later, I dropped over at Richardson's and Michaels' place to hang out for a while. When I got there I knocked, but no one answered. I noticed that the door was unlocked, so I let myself in. I was sitting on the couch watching TV when, all of a sudden, Richardson walked out of his bedroom naked, wrapped in a sheet. Turns out he and Michaels had two girls over and the four of them were in the middle of enjoying an orgy. After greeting me, he went back into his bedroom and closed the door behind him.

Five minutes later, an enticing female emerged from Richardson's bedroom dressed only in a pair of white lace panties. She walked over to where I was seated and stood there before me with her arms crossed over her breasts. She asked if I would like to join the orgy. At that moment I realized she was the girl I'd recently met at the motel party. Needless to say, I joyfully accepted her invitation. Her name was Connie and her friend's name was Carrie. I learned that, although they were not exclusive, Connie and Michaels had an ongoing relationship.

In the late fall of 1972, English superstar David Bowie, his wife Angela and Bowie's manager, Tony Defries, arrived in Michigan. They were there to visit Iggy Pop in his hometown of Ann Arbor. Bowie had developed a strong interest in Iggy and persuaded his manager to help boost Iggy's career. During their stay, Angela somehow met Richardson, and they immediately fell into a romantic relationship. When Bowie and Defries left to return to England, Angela remained behind in Ann Arbor and moved in with Richardson and Michaels.

Angela Bowie was a brash and seductive bisexual predator, and even though I'm sure Richardson truly found her attractive, I think he may have viewed her as his ticket to stardom. He appointed her manager of The Fallen Angels and was convinced that with her influence and connections, she'd be able to help us land a record deal.

For whatever their reasons, Richardson and Angela would put on outrageous displays of public affection. I found their over-the-top, love-struck behavior disgusting. Once I made the mistake of taking the two of them with me to the Northville Downs harness racing track. Angela was dressed in what looked like a lace-up tutu, and had a long pinkish orange feathered boa draped around her neck. We were in the mezzanine area, and while I was trying to form the races, they were sitting next to me, their legs entangled, passionately kissing and groping each other. It was extremely distracting and annoying. Mind you, we were at the fucking track!

Despite the fact that I found Angela's loud and flamboyant personality disturbing, I did my best to get along with her. One day, as a friendly gesture, I invited her to go with me to a porn theater to see Deep Throat, and she accepted. During the movie, she sat pressed against me with her head on my shoulder, and I'm sure had I asked her, she would have been more than willing to give me a blowjob. But she was Richardson's girl so I decided not to go for it.

Though totally absorbed in our music and rock and roll lifestyle, we couldn't play out and earn money because we didn't have a full-time guitarist. Until now I had stolen and borrowed what I needed to get by, but at this point, I was falling behind on the rent and could no longer afford my apartment. Richardson and Michaels were in the same boat and on the verge of eviction. Connie and Carrie were renting a house together in Redford, and fortunately, when they learned of our circumstances, they offered to let us live with them rent-free. Soon, Richardson, Angela, Michaels, and I moved in and set up living quarters in the basement.

Almost immediately, Angela, attracted to both sexes, began an insistent barrage of unwelcome sexual advances toward Connie and Carrie. Though Angela knew they weren't bisexual, her behavior became so obnoxious and offensive, the girls finally had to tell her to back off. By this time, I was becoming more and more infatuated with Connie. When I decided to let her know my feelings, she told me she felt the same way. A short while later I moved up from her basement to her bedroom.

In early 1973, Angela announced that she was flying to New York to spend a couple of days with her still-husband, David Bowie and their baby, Zowie Bowie at the Chelsea, a well-known stomping ground for famous artists, writers, and musicians. She told us we were more than welcome to stay with them in their suite. Richardson was unable to go for some reason or another, but Michaels and I decided to tag along. Shortly after we checked in, Bowie showed up. He was in the Ziggy Stardust phase of his career and when he entered the suite, he was outfitted as though he had just stepped off the stage, flamboyant in a glittery jumpsuit and platform shoes, a zombie-like complexion, shaved eyebrows, and spiked scarlet hair. He was accompanied by a nanny who had baby Bowie in tow.

A few minutes after he arrived, I ducked into the bedroom and through the open door, I could see that in the living area, celebrity guests were pouring in to pay homage to the legendary rock icon. He was seated on a throne-like chair surrounded by friends looking like a king holding court. Among those who came by were Marilyn Monroe look-alike, Cyrinda Foxe, and members of the glam band, New York Dolls. Later that night, in spite of the fact that the nanny had already gone home for the evening, Angela and David decided to go out on the town, leaving Michaels and me behind to babysit their kid. We didn't know what the hell we were doing, and we couldn't get Zowie to stop bawling. Eventually, our prayers were answered and the little brat cried himself to sleep.

At the same time we were in NYC, The Alice Cooper group was in town preparing for a massive world tour to promote their new album, *Billion Dollar Babies*. Their manager, Shep Gordon, whom I had met a few times before, had an office in the city, so I decided to call him to see if I could get in touch with Alice. When I phoned Shep's office, Alice happened to be there, and he got on the line and invited me to a dress rehearsal scheduled for that afternoon.

I, together with Michaels, went to a large practice facility and watched in fascination as Alice and his band rehearsed on their newly constructed, massive, multi-level, state-of-the-art portable stage. This awe-inspiring structure was equipped with all the elaborate trademark stage props Alice used for his gory and outrageous theatrical performances, including an electric chair, guillotine, and gallows. From the stage to the props, everything was the best that money could buy. They really had become "Billion Dollar Babies!"

After rehearsal, we were to meet Alice for drinks at a popular New York City watering hole. When we arrived, we found him at a table with comedy greats George Burns and Jack Benny. Although Alice was on an extremely tight schedule, he still made time to hang with us for a while. He truly was, and I'm certain still is, a very kind and considerate guy.

Alice had brought his friend, Jimmy Optner, along with him to the bar. Optner, a drummer and former member of the Detroit-based band, Catfish, was to house-sit that night at Alice's luxurious Manhattan penthouse apartment while Alice was staying elsewhere. After Alice left, Optner, Michaels, and I went clubbing and picked up a sizzling hot, six-foot tall southern babe who called herself Miss Alabama. We took her back to Alice's penthouse and the four of us climbed into his bed (sorry Vince). While I was naked on top of Miss Alabama making out with her, I suddenly felt someone licking my asshole (and it *obviously* wasn't Miss Alabama). Panic-stricken, I shrieked and bolted off the bed and out of the bedroom. To this day, I maintain a don't-ask-don't-tell policy as to the identity of the offender.

On the evening of Friday, March 9, 1973, The Fallen Angels played their first concert at the United Dairy Workers Hall-Local 83, located on Second Avenue between 6 Mile and Davison. We decided beforehand that we wanted to adopt a glam-band look for the show. So that afternoon, Connie took me to a beauty parlor where a stylist bleached out several strips of my hair and then replaced the color with temporary hair dye in pink, silver, and turquoise. My locks looked spectacular and totally outrageous. Getting ready for the show, we all put on lipstick, eye shadow, and other makeup. This concert was not only very important to the band, but also to Connie and Carrie, and the girls got all decked out for the special occasion. (Side note: when I showered the next day, all the dye washed out of my hair and the bleached areas had become damaged and frizzy, leaving me looking like a collie in heat.)

We elected to use guitarist Terry Kelly for the concert which, due to his constant intake of heroin, was a risky move that almost backfired. He was so high during our performance that he was unable to stand for long periods and had to play most of the set seated on a stool. Halfway through our show, Kelly's guitar pickup, which was held in by a cigarette butt, fell out of his guitar, and we were forced to stop for several minutes while he fumbled around putting it back in place. Despite this, the crowd's response was decent, and we were rewarded with cheers after each song.

Following our performance, I abandoned Connie and hooked up with Evelyn, a young stripper I knew and liked who had attended the concert. From the venue we went back to her house and spent the night together. Connie was devastated. (I know, I know...what a dick-move, literally and figuratively.) The next day I apologized to Connie and she was somehow able to forgive me for my betrayal.

A few weeks later, Angela set up an audition for The Fallen Angels with several big-time New York record producers. We had to find someplace fast to showcase the band, and on such short notice, the only place we were able to secure was a low-class strip joint in a downtrodden area of West Detroit. As a result of the recent Terry Kelly fiasco, this time we utilized the services of guitarists Ray Goodman and Mike Nardone (Nardone was a promising up-and-comer and hometown friend of Richard Michaels). We all had high hopes that this would be our big break. Disappointingly though, only one executive showed up (who knows if he even was a record producer), and he expressed no interest in signing our band. This setback, coupled with the fact that we had no other prospects of a record deal on the horizon, caused me to lose faith in the band, and a week later I quit.

Richardson and Michaels kept The Fallen Angels together and moved to Los Angeles to further pursue a recording contract. They eventually parted ways with Angela Bowie and were signed by a talent agency, GTO Productions, which was co-owned and co-operated by Warren Entner, a former member of The Grass Roots. They brought in Michaels' friend, guitarist Mike Nardone, and split the drumming duties between Thom Mooney and Jack White. Thom Mooney had some pedigree as a former member of Todd Rundgren's group Nazz. Jack White later went on to play with Rick Springfield (and also married actress Katey Sagal, co-star of the Fox sitcom, *Married with Children*). The re-formed group lasted for a year or so, but was never able to land a record deal. Ultimately, The Fallen Angels did what fallen angels do: plummeted, crashed, and burned.

Afterwards, Richard Michaels remained in LA and joined a band called Alien Project. The group included Craig Krampf on drums, Steve DeLacey on guitar, and a destined-for-stardom Steve Perry on lead vocals. Alien Project produced a demo tape that led to great interest from several major labels. Michaels sent a copy of the demo to Nardone, who in turn made a copy for me. Songs on the demo included, "If You Need Me, Call Me," "My, My, My," "Special Kind Of Love," and "Makes No Difference." I was completely knocked out when I heard it. Steve Perry's voice was incredibly full and rich, blending perfectly with Michaels'. The band was exceptional, and every song sounded like a top ten hit.

Later, in the summer of '77, Alien Project would be less than a week away from signing a deal with Columbia Records when, on the 4th of July, Michaels was killed in a car accident. I've read that his death had such a devastating impact on Perry that he broke up the band and returned to his family in the San Joaquin Valley while he reconsidered his music career.

In the meantime, the San Francisco-based group, Journey, was in the process of making a musical change following the lack of success of their first three albums. A VP at Columbia Records, who was aware of this, sent Journey's manager a copy of the Alien Project demo. One thing led to another and in a short time, in great part because of this demo, Perry became the lead singer of Journey, and of course, the rest is rock and roll history. In April of 1984, Steve Perry released his first solo album, *Street Talk*, and dedicated it to the memory of Richard Michaels.

My friend and bandmate, Richard Haddad Michaels, devoted his life toward building a successful musical career, and had finally reached an important milestone on his path. It saddens me that he never got the chance to complete *his* journey.

Chapter Twelve:
Lost in the Struggle

I found myself, once again, living at my mom's one-bedroom apartment, sleeping on the sofa bed in the living room. I had no money or prospects, so I decided to chance my arm at betting the horses. But I needed a stake, and the only possession I owned of any value was my made-to-order set of green sparkle Ludwig drums. Begrudgingly, I put them up for sale and Sonny Cingolani's brother-in-law, Johnny Sarkisian, practically stole them for $500. I lost it all at the racetrack in less than a week. Soon after, I had one of the most harrowing theft-related experiences of my life.

In the dark hours of a cold and snowy April morning, two friends and I were out burglarizing gas service stations. Our method of operation, which had a proven track record, was quick and really quite simple. We'd drive around searching for out-of-the-way, closed-for-the-night service stations. When we'd spot one that looked good, my guys would drop me off on a nearby street and park on the side of the road to serve as lookouts. When the coast was clear they'd signal me by flashing the headlights. I'd then sneak up to the building, kick out a small pane of glass from the service bay door and quickly crawl through. I'd steal the fifty to seventy-five dollars typically left in the cash register overnight for the next day's business. It only took a few minutes to commit these petty heists. I never took time looking for anything else to steal; I wanted to get in and out as fast as possible.

After having successfully hit three service stations already that morning, I was just about finished thieving a fourth, when cops came swinging into the station; I guess I must have triggered a silent alarm. In the split-second after I'd crawled out the broken window and stood, I was looking at two police officers not more than fifty feet away with their weapons drawn and aimed at me. Instinctively, I decided to run for it. As I fled into the large wooded area behind the service station, I heard a cop yell, "Halt or I'll shoot!" but, moronically, I didn't stop. An instant later, I took a tumble and fell face first onto the ground. At that moment, I heard a loud pop and felt a bullet whiz past my head. It was chilling to realize I was now running for my life.

After I'd gone a mile or so, I came upon a small residential neighborhood. I made my way stealthily through the neighborhood by ducking behind snow-covered bushes and beneath vehicles parked on the sleet-covered streets. I had just crawled under a pickup truck when I spotted a patrol car creeping slowly down the road, shining a spotlight on and between each house as it passed by. With the cruiser nearing the pickup truck, I held my breath, prepared for the worst. Miraculously, the patrol car rolled past the truck and disappeared around a curve. Shivering with cold and fear, I slid out from under the truck and continued on, moving silently and deliberately, making use of every piece of cover as I approached another wooded area.

Eventually, I saw beyond the trees a well-traveled, four-lane road, and at the risk of being seen, crept out of the woods to the shoulder and peeked right and left. Less than a mile away in each direction, police cars with flashing lights blocked the road. I hit the ground and wormed my way across the cold damp street on my belly, somehow managing to make it to the other side without being detected. Then, I ran and walked for about a mile or so to the next major highway, and from there, half-frozen and soaked in melted snow, I hitchhiked my way home. The next day when I contacted my boys, I was relieved to hear they were able to slip away from the scene unnoticed, and they were absolutely amazed to hear that I also managed to make a clean getaway. Honestly, so was I. After this near-disastrous undertaking, I decided it might be time to start cutting back on my criminal activity a bit. I chuckled to myself as I mused that if I ever were to quit for good, the crime rate in Detroit might actually drop a percentage point or two.

I needed to put together another band. I met with my friend, Tim Rice, a booking agent for Gail & Rice talent agency, a long-established and well-respected entertainment company co-founded by his father, and he agreed to help me by offering the use of his office facility for rehearsals. I persuaded my long-time pal and bassist, Al Zsenyuk, to get involved in the project. From there, Tim, Al, and I, were able to assemble some of the more gifted musicians and singers in the Detroit area, including guitarist, Ray Goodman, with whom I had previously worked in The Fallen Angels; Drew Abbott, former guitarist for Third Power, a popular Detroit-based band; Marcy Levy, a young and rising rhythm and blues singer; and solid background vocalists, Wendy Pooley and Marsha Pritchard.

Someone came up with the band name, "Hammer," and it stuck. Zsenyuk let me borrow an old secondhand set of silver sparkle Ludwig drums, as I had sold mine for track money. Hammer practiced a couple times and came up with a handful of well-constructed songs, highlighted by a burning version of the old soul classic "Way Back Home." Unfortunately, the band never played out and only lasted a few months, which was a shame considering its outstanding group of talent. In 1974, Drew Abbott would form The Silver Bullet Band with Bob Seger, and Marcy Levy (aka Marcella Detroit) joined Eric Clapton's group.

I'd heard that Bob Seger was about to go on tour but needed both a drummer and bass player. I mentioned it to Zsenyuk and bet him I could make us members of his backup band. Zsenyuk was unconvinced, so to prove to him that it was indeed possible, I arranged through Seger's manager, Punch Andrews, for whom The Knightriders had once auditioned, to meet with Seger at his residence in Mt Clemens, just north of Detroit. (I wonder now if Punch felt he owed me one for shtupping my mother.)

The next day, Al and I got together with Seger, and with only a brief discussion, were invited to join his band. Driving home that night, I began to have second thoughts about the situation. I still didn't own a drum kit and with rehearsals beginning at Seger's house the following week, I was again going to have to borrow Zsenyuk's cheap-assed, piece-of-shit drums. Adding to that, I wasn't familiar with the material on Seger's more recent albums. And to make matters worse, I was concerned that Al, who'd never before played or toured with a big-name act, might not be enough of a musician to take on this challenge.

The first two rehearsals were held with just me, Al, and Rick Mannassa, Seger's regular keyboard player. As I had presumed, I'd never heard most of the numbers we were working on. Knowing that Mannassa had quickly picked up that I was winging it, my confidence tumbled and my playing went to shit.

At the next rehearsal, Seger joined us and sang and played guitar. We went over several of his hit songs, but the band wasn't tight and I could tell by the look on Seger's face that he was disappointed. When the rehearsal ended, I told Al I thought we would probably be canned. That night, Seger called me and said he felt that my chops were down and that, unfortunately, he wouldn't be able to include me in his upcoming tour. Although I half expected this, his words felt like daggers piercing my soul. I idolized Seger and felt that I was now lowered in his eyes. But what stung even more was learning a few days later that Seger was keeping Zsenyuk. Nowadays, when young musicians ask me for advice, I speak of this experience and strongly recommend to them that, just like a devout boy scout: "Always be prepared." If I could do it over again, I'd make sure I had every Seger song down cold before pursuing a position in his band.

This being a low point in my life, I began suffering bouts of severe anxiety. I experienced recurring panic attacks and acquired the nervous habit of sticking my hair in my mouth and chewing on it. I also found I could no longer go to restaurants because it felt like the patrons were staring at me. These and other neurotic behaviors led me to a self-prescribed regimen of Valium. Thankfully, over time, these debilitating disorders gradually diminished.

After moping around for a bit, my ego kicked in, and I decided it was time to get back in the game. With help from my mother, I managed to put enough cash together to purchase a set of navy-blue Premier drums, and for the next few months, I practiced for hours every day. Once I got my chops back, my confidence returned and, with renewed energy and a vengeance, I set out to once again join a band.

I ran into bassist Gary Beam with whom I had previously played in The Lavender Hill Mob. He told me that he was in a bar band called Marcus (named for the lead singer), and they were looking for a replacement for their drummer, who was soon to leave the group. He asked me to come see them play, and the following weekend I went to a lounge to check them out. They covered an assortment of top forty tunes highlighted by a featured medley of Doobie Brothers songs. Their drummer was excellent and by far the strongest musician in the band, but the other guys weren't bad at all. In addition to lead singer, Marcus Malone and bass player, Beam, the band consisted of Tom Curry on keys, Gene Bloch on guitar, and their exceptional drummer, whose name I can't recall.

I spoke with the band on a break between sets and learned that they were managed by Joe Peraino, who was a staff producer at Motown Records and former guitarist for a Detroit-based band called Power of Zeus. I also learned that the band was tired of working bars and had a mutual desire to play concerts and perform strictly original material. They were quite aware of my musical and performance credentials, and before I left that night, they asked me to join their band

and help guide them toward their goal. I felt they were sincere and had potential, so I accepted their offer.

I took the band under my wing and by utilizing all that I had learned from playing with Ted Nugent and The Amboy Dukes, I helped transform them from a mere cover group to a genuine and original rock and roll concert band. I gave them detailed instructions on how to open and close a show and how to carry themselves on stage. I helped them create full-on rock music arrangements, and I even wrote an original song (words and melody) for the band, a power ballad called "Kelly." This song was actually written about my ex-girlfriend, Wendy, but it felt too personal to name it after her.

Our first concert was just outside Detroit at the old Melody Theater in Inkster. We played a kickass set and the audience ate us up. We were actually called back for not one, but two encores. In a relatively short period of time, we had made a significant amount of progress. Meanwhile, Joe Peraino approached Curry, Beam, Bloch, and me to record a studio album with a blues guitarist named Luther Allison. Downplaying the offer, he said it wouldn't take more than a couple of days and we'd be paid $200 bucks a piece. Without giving it a second thought, we all agreed to do it. A day before the first session, I was blown away to learn that Allison was signed to Motown Records, and that the recording was to take place at the legendary Hitsville USA, Motown's first recording studio! Luther Allison, I later learned, recorded on Motown's Gordy label, and was the only blues guitarist Motown ever signed.

I still remember stepping into the old but well-kept white and blue house-turned-recording-studio at 2648 West Grand Boulevard in downtown Detroit. I was in the center of the famous Studio A, where legends such as Stevie Wonder and Marvin Gaye had stood and recorded their hits. Berry Gordy, Jr. had christened the house Hitsville USA, which is now home to the Motown Historical Museum, one of Detroit's most popular tourist attractions.

We cut seven songs in two days: "Someday Pretty Baby," "Easy Baby," "Part Time Love," "Now You Got It," "Let's Have A Little Talk," "Driving Wheel," and "Into My Life," all of which made it onto Allison's 1974 album, *Luther's Blues*. Of interesting note, the drum track on "Someday Pretty Baby," a song co-written by Berry Gordy and recorded by Singin' Sammy Ward, was created in an unconventional way. A recording engineer played Ward's original version through my headphones and taped me while I played along with the record. The result was a perfect track and on the first take, no less.

Two of the finest and funkiest numbers on this album, "Now You Got It" and "Into My Life," were written and arranged on the spot by Allison, Block, Beam and me. I'm very proud of my performance on this album and believe it to be some of the best session work I've done. Sadly, Luther Allison passed away in July of 1997, and *Luther's Blues* was re-released on February 27, 2001. Happily, I'm still receiving royalty checks from *Luther's Blues* through EMI Music Publishing from Jobete Music Co., Inc. Yet, come to think of it, I haven't seen a penny in royalties from Nugent's *Survival Of The Fittest* in over forty-five years. Some things just make you go hmmmm …???

Just when things were looking up, Connie, with whom I was still very much involved, called and said she had something important to tell me. Can you guess what it was? No, she wasn't pregnant. I went to see her at her parents' house (she was once again living at home), and when I arrived, she sat me down and began to cry. She told me that over the weekend she had been at a party, gotten falling-down drunk, and slept with Marcus, the singer in my band. My blood began to boil. I wasn't naïve; I recognized Connie's complicity in the matter. What really bothered me was Marcus' betrayal. He knew Connie and I were going together and so she was off limits to him. I suspected that he may have taken advantage of her drunken condition. As furious as I was, I almost broke out in laughter when Connie told me that just before they did it, Marcus removed his wig, and she realized with shock that he was actually bald. The next day I called the band together (Marcus was a no-show) and quit without revealing the reason.

Some three years later, unbeknownst to me at the time, Marcus landed a record deal with United Artists Records and released a self-titled album, *Marcus*. I found out about it one day when I noticed it on sale at a record store. I purchased a copy and discovered that my song, "Kelly" was on the album. The label credits acknowledged me as "Kelly" songwriter; however, Marcus, Bloch and Curry were also credited for writing the song. This was a disturbing surprise since Marcus had never received my signed or verbal permission to record the song, let alone add his name to it as a co-writer. I still can't figure out how he got this past United Artist Records' legal department. I have no idea the number of copies sold, but I received no compensation for my contribution to this album whatsoever. For what it's worth, I have to give it to Marcus that the record was really quite good, and the musicianship was strong and solid.

On the other hand, I have to laugh at Marcus, because he screwed up the lyrics on the second chorus of "Kelly." Instead of "Just a skinny girl with a pretty face," Marcus got tongue twisted and sang, "Just a pretty girl with a skinny face." All I can say is…"Dude, at least you could have gotten the friggin' words right, you backstabbing, meat-headed shit-sack!"

Chapter Thirteen: New Beginnings

_In_ 1970, my dad and Jan had disbanded The Debutantes and moved to Las Vegas in order to better pursue Jan's career as a solo artist. One day out of the blue, I received a call from my grandmother, Ruthie, who lived in a mobile home in Farmington Hills. She told me that my father had snuck into Detroit for the weekend and that he wanted to meet with me. This was somewhat of a risky move on his part, considering there was an open warrant for his arrest in the state of Michigan for nonpayment of alimony and child support. The intensity of the hatred and resentment I felt for him had increased over the years, and I struggled with the idea of seeing him again. I downed a half bottle of bourbon and spent a sleepless night mulling it over. The following afternoon, in a state of hangover, I picked up Connie and went over to my grandmother's to meet with my dad.

When I came face to face with him, my hostility took over and I unleashed a barrage of insults and expletives at him. He took me to a room at the back of the trailer where we could talk alone, and eventually, I calmed down. Dad started out by telling me he was sorry for the way things had turned out, and that he wanted to try and repair our relationship. He added that he and Jan had recently moved from Las Vegas to Hollywood. Then, out of left field, he stunned me by asking: "Will you come and live with us in Los Angeles?" I then stunned myself by instantly replying, "Yes, but only if Connie can come with me." He thought for a moment and then agreed, so I told him that I would talk it over with Connie and get back to him. On the way home I told Connie about my dad's offer and right before dropping her off I said, "If I go and join my father in California, will you come along with me?" She responded with an enthusiastic, "Yes!"

On a Friday in November of 1973, Connie and I excitedly boarded a plane for our cross-country flight toward new beginnings. All we brought along were some essentials, my drums, and the only cash we had between us, $750. The plan was to connect with my father in Las Vegas, where Jan was performing in the "Bare-bary Coast Review" at the Bonanza Hotel, spend the weekend, and then all of us would continue on to Hollywood. In true K J Knight fashion, within forty-eight hours of our arrival in Vegas, I managed to gamble away every last cent of our money; when we touched down in Los Angeles, we were flat broke.

The reason my dad and Jan had decided to relocate to Hollywood was for Jan to take professional acting lessons in hopes of landing a role in a soap opera or film. My dad had gone ahead of her to prepare the way and was working as a manager for an apartment building located directly behind Mann's (Grauman's) Chinese Theatre. As compensation along with his salary, he was permitted to live in one of the apartments, rent-free. Though Jan eventually joined my father in Hollywood, she was rarely around, commuting regularly to Las Vegas to perform at various hotel lounges and casinos. I suspected that one of the reasons my father had asked me to move in with him was because he was lonely.

In the beginning, Connie and I lived with my dad and Jan in their apartment. Dad immediately hired me as assistant manager and printed up apartment business cards, listing both of our names. My primary duties were maintaining the swimming pool, sweeping the parking garage, and cleaning-up apartments after tenants moved out. Connie assisted me by doing the lion's share of the apartment clean-ups. (The poor thing got stuck with the short end of the stick.) Soon after starting this new job, Connie and I were able to move into an apartment of our own in the building.

Many aspiring actors lived at the apartments, including Sherman Hemsley, who, at the time, had just been awarded the role of George Jefferson on the hit television show, *All in the Family*. My father introduced me to him one day, and when I mentioned that I was a musician, he extended an open invitation to come to his apartment to listen to the newly-released Yes album. Later, my dad, ever the homophobe, warned me not to go, because Hemsley was rumored to be gay. As I became reacquainted with my old man, it became clear that he hadn't changed a bit. So, it didn't surprise me when I learned that, for a piece of the action, he was letting a pimp named Zeon operate a prostitution ring out of the apartments.

Jan was an animal rights activist and had taken in at least a dozen stray cats and dogs over the years. However, she was seldom around to take care of them and expected my dad to handle it. My father had neither the time nor the desire to tend to any animals, so, when Jan was away, he'd locked them up for days or weeks at a time in a small storage unit enclosed by chain-link fence located in the underground parking area.

Occasionally, he'd assign either me or Connie the task of going down to storage to feed the animals. Those poor, half-wild, half-crazed creatures would fight tooth and claw for every morsel we provided. So, rather than opening the gate for fear of being scratched or bitten, we would quickly push the pet food and scraps through openings in the chain-link fence, and then step away from the frenzy. What was even more messed up was that shortly before the occasions that Jan was due to arrive home from Vegas for a few days, we would have to help my dad round up all of her pets and put them back in the apartment so that she was none the wiser.

The adventure that Connie and I had set out on had strengthened our bond. I realized I was sincerely in love with her, and she with me. Not long after we moved to California, I drove her in my dad's Cadillac to an employment interview she had scored in downtown Los Angeles for a clerical position at Bank of America. She got the job. On the way home, sitting in stop-and-go traffic on the 101 Freeway, I asked for her hand in marriage, and she accepted.

Connie put me in charge of the wedding arrangements… what was she thinking? I wasn't familiar with Los Angeles or the surrounding areas. From the Yellow Pages, I randomly chose the Lily of the Valley Wedding Chapel in the nearby neighborhood of Watts for our ceremony. I asked Gary Beam (my bandmate from The Lavender Hill Mob and Marcus) who had recently moved to Hollywood with his wife Mari, to be my best man, and Connie asked Mari to be her maid of honor. For the wedding, I wore a purple velvet suit coat, a yellow cowboy shirt, and green bellbottom pants. Connie wore a sexy full-length purple gown that she'd purchased at Frederick's of Hollywood, famously known for its provocative lingerie.

On March 2, 1974, Connie and I were driven by my dad and Jan to our wedding with Gary and Mari following behind. As we neared the chapel, we began noticing graffiti-marked buildings, boarded up houses, and loud drunks meandering the streets. It soon became clear that the Lily of the Valley Wedding Chapel was located in a rough, run-down section of South-Central Los Angeles. Arriving at the chapel, as the six of us interlopers stepped out of our cars, we got quite a few double-takes from the locals. Our wedding ceremony was short and sweet. The reception was held at our apartment, and almost all of our fellow tenants attended, including Sherman Hemsley, who gave us a rubber tree plant as a wedding gift.

Prior to relocating to Hollywood, my father had lived in Las Vegas for a few years working at a collection agency called Credit Associates. He had done well there and was highly esteemed by the owners of the company. The firm had recently opened an office in Century City, Los Angeles, at 1900 Avenue of the Stars, and contacted my dad with an offer to manage it. He accepted, quit his management job at the apartments, and the four of us (plus all of Jan's pets) moved out and rented a house on Omelveny Avenue in Sun Valley, just outside Los Angeles.

A month or so after Dad started his new job, he persuaded Connie and me to come work for him. He brought me on as a bill collector and her as a bookkeeper. I had never had a desk job, didn't look the part, and certainly had no proper business clothes to wear. So, to fit in at the office, I wore a short-haired wig and dressed in my dad's extra-large collared shirts and pre-tied ties. With my dad's training, I developed a knack for the collection business and was soon promoted to assistant manager over approximately twelve staff employees. Our largest client was a mail order company, Fingerhut, based in St Cloud, Minnesota. We also collected unpaid gambling markers for Las Vegas hotel casinos.

I'd heard that Ike and Tina Turner were holding open auditions for drummers at a recording studio in Los Angeles and thought, "Why not give it a try?" and so I did. On the day of the audition, the lobby of the studio was packed full of hopeful drummers; I was later told that over a hundred drummers had shown up. When it was time for my audition, I was ushered into the studio where I took a seat behind a small set of drums, consisting of only a bass drum, snare drum, and hi-hat. A voice from the control room piped up, "Are you ready?" and I nodded. As "Proud Mary" started playing through the studio speakers, I began playing along. When the song was over, the voice spoke to me again: "Thank you. Leave us your name and number and we'll get back to you."

I figured that was probably the end of it. But, a couple days later, I got a call from an Ike and Tina Turner representative asking me to return for a second audition. This time, when I was led into the studio, I noticed there was now a black upright acoustic piano situated next to the same set of drums. A moment after I sat down at the kit, in walked Ike "Pistol Whippin'" Turner. Without a word, he seated himself at the piano, snorted a fat rail of coke, and started banging out a song. I joined in with a simple, uncluttered groove, and it was going quite well until I decided to show off a little bit by playing a busier, syncopated beat. This turned out to be a bad move, because Ike suddenly stopped playing and uttered with a scowl, "Thanks anyway." I learned a very important lesson that day: sometimes less is more.

I found out that The Stooges, featuring one-of-a-kind frontman Iggy Pop, guitarist Ron Asheton, and bassist Jimmy Recca, were living in West Hollywood at the Coronet Apartments on the Sunset Strip. When I'd played with Nugent, our paths had crossed a few times, but I never really got to know them personally. One afternoon, I impulsively went up to their fourth-story apartment, knocked on the door and reintroduced myself. They remembered me and enthusiastically invited me in.

We hit it off well, and before I left, they informed me that Doors manager, Danny Sugarman, was searching for someone to take the place of the late great Jim Morrison, and that Danny believed Iggy could be Mr. Mojo Risin's heir apparent. They added that the three of them were going to jam at Sugarman's place later in the week with Doors keyboardist, Ray Manzarek, and asked if I wanted to come and rock out with them. Naturally, I jumped at the chance.

Sugarman's house was located on Wonderland Avenue in Laurel Canyon. (In 1981, the gruesome murders involving porn-star John Holmes, better known as Johnny Wadd, took place at a house on this notorious street.) At the time, Iggy was hooked on heroin and extremely undependable. When he didn't show up, we went ahead and jammed anyway without him. It was a unique honor to play with these distinguished rock musicians, Manzarek and Asheton. Each had his own recognizable and distinctive style. Manzarek, with his endless array of improvised melodic lines, crossed with Ashton's raw simplified driving riffs, took the music through some wondrous twists and turns.

We didn't finish playing until after midnight and I was pretty beat, so when I took off, I left my drums overnight at Sugarman's house. The next day when I came for them, I could tell that someone had been playing on them and had placed a large, heavy, dirt-covered boulder inside the bass drum to prevent it from sliding. This was both disrespectful and stupid, as the drum could have easily been damaged. I demanded that Sugarman tell me who'd done it, and he sheepishly told me that Hunt Sales, one of Soupy Sales' kids, had come by after I left, and Sugarman had allowed him to mess around with my drums. I've never forgotten what that dumbass Hunt did, and if I ever catch up with him, I'm gonna smash a shaving cream pie in his fuckin' face!

After the Manzarek jam, I was thrilled to be asked to join up with The Stooges. We worked on three or four original numbers that Asheton had written, including "The Mombasa Flip." I remember thinking to myself that his songs, musically speaking, were very basic and hardly a challenge to play, but I also understood that there was a genius to the simplicity of them. Things were going pretty smoothly for me with this band, except for one huge frustrating problem: Iggy, our lead singer, rarely showed up for practices. Worse than that, on some nights, Iggy, in a drugged stupor, would pass out somewhere on the beach and not turn up for days.

One day, following an early afternoon rehearsal that Iggy actually attended, I persuaded him to come with me to the Hollywood Park Racetrack by promising that if I won anything, I'd split it with him. Iggy had on a pair of jeans that were ripped wide open from his crotch to his knees and he wasn't wearing any underwear; whenever he leaned forward his package was on full display. Inside the racetrack, while I made my selections, Iggy went wandering around the clubhouse drawing appalled stares from those members of the betting public he encountered. We were only there for maybe three races before I lost all my money.

On the way back to Iggy's, we stopped at my house to get something to eat, and I told him he could help himself. As Iggy was bent over perusing the selections in the refrigerator, my old man walked into the kitchen getting an eyeful of Iggy raiding the fridge with his dick hanging out. Repulsed, my dad blurted out, "Who the fuck *are* you?" Then he grabbed me and took me aside and said, "Get this fuckin' weirdo outta here!"

I was more than conscious of Iggy's potential and star power, but due to his ever-present drug addiction and erratic and unreliable behavior, I felt that a future in a band with him would be futile. I suggested to the other members that they cut ties with Iggy and re-form by replacing him with vocalist, Dave Gilbert, with whom I had played in The Amboy Dukes. Ron Asheton felt as I did and intimated that he was ready to try something different.

Asheton began plans to form a new band, a hybrid version of The Stooges he named The New Order with me and Jimmy Recca. He must have been planning to make this move for some time, as he had already selected someone to manage the group. Asheton and his manager were very serious about this arrangement and had me accompany them to a bank to sign a personal management agreement witnessed by a notary public.

Not more than a month or so later, I left the band as it appeared to me that it would never get off the ground. I didn't learn until many years later that Gilbert, my vocalist recommendation, had in fact, joined The New Order and that in 1977 the band released an album on RCA's Fun Records/Isadora Label entitled *Declaration of War*. As for Iggy Pop, he eventually beat his heroin habit and went on to carve out his illustrious career.

The Alice Cooper Group had recently split up, and Alice was in the process of piecing together a new band for a worldwide concert tour to promote his first solo album, *Welcome to My Nightmare*. Cooper was living a life fit for a king, owning no fewer than four homes: a penthouse apartment in Manhattan; a mansion in Greenwich, Connecticut; a modern house in Phoenix, Arizona; and a mountain palace in the Hollywood Hills. At some point, I got wind that he was at home in Hollywood and decided to risk paying him an unsolicited visit with the sole purpose of asking if he might consider hiring me into his band. I have to admit I felt a bit like a stalker, but I was on a mission this day. Alice was nice enough to see me, and after we talked awhile, I managed to muster the courage to ask him what I'd come for. I'll never forget his answer. He said, "K J you're a funk drummer, and I don't play that style of music." Then he added, "If I ever do record a funky song, you're second in line as drummer behind Buddy Miles." That's not the answer I was looking for, but at least he was honest with me.

Meanwhile, Connie and I were making good salaries including employee benefits at Credit Associates, and it wasn't long before we were able to get a vehicle and a place of our own. We bought a pre-owned gold Dodge Dart and found a nice apartment at a Spanish-colonial building in Santa Monica. We even had cable TV! We decided it was a good time to start working on the baby we wanted, and we got pregnant the first month we tried. This was one of the happiest times of our lives.

One Monday morning at work, my father called Connie and me into his office and closed the door behind us. He sat us down and told us that for some time he'd had a feeling that Jan was having an affair, but he had no proof. He explained that, over the past weekend, he had gone to Vegas unannounced and learned that she was spending an unacceptable amount of time with a local lounge musician about her age. He informed us that when he'd confronted her with his suspicions, she responded by asking for a divorce; he agreed straight away. As he continued to talk, I began to detect a growing happiness inside myself that this senseless marriage, which had over the years caused my mother and me so much grief and hardship, was finally coming to an end. Shortly after their divorce, with my dad no longer available to prop up her professional life, Jan's career fizzled faster than a pissed-on sparkler at a July 4th picnic, and in the end, she never amounted to much of anything.

For a brief while, my father had the audacity to try to woo back my mother. After a series of long-distance phone calls, she agreed to meet him in Los Angeles to discuss a possible reconciliation. They never did reunite, but not long after my parents' rendezvous, my mother moved to Los Angeles and secured a job as a cashier at the famous Chasen's Restaurant in Beverly Hills, a hangout for entertainment luminaries, where she worked for more than a decade.

Leaving his job at Credit Associates, my dad moved back to Michigan with the intent of resurrecting his once highly profitable collection company and to be close to his mother,

Ruthie, who was dying of cancer. On his return, he took a management job at the Botsford Place Terrace Apartments in Farmington Hills, located behind the Botsford General Hospital, and, on the side, began rebuilding his business. He also reconnected with his old band buddy, Joe Oddo, who was still active in music and leading a wedding quartet. Oddo, like my father, had left his wife for a much younger woman, the vocalist in his band. They were married with one baby and another on the way.

Oddo had three daughters from his first marriage, the youngest of whom was 21-year-old Sarah. She was an insulin-dependent, brittle diabetic, who faced a shortened life expectancy. Joe introduced my dad to Sarah one day when he came to Joe's house for a visit; Dad became attracted to her. Then, my old man did the unthinkable: he began an affair with his best friend's daughter. They managed to keep it secret for a month or so, but after a while, my dad and Sarah began openly dating, and eventually she moved in with him. When Joe got word, he was incensed and never spoke to his daughter or my dad again.

Chapter Fourteen:
Back Home Again

$\mathcal{I}$n the winter of 1975, a pregnant Connie and I each came down with severe cases of homesickness, and decided to return to the Motor City. On my father's advice, we moved into an apartment across the hall from his. I immediately teamed up with my old sidekick, Sonny Cingolani, and we put together a show band called Las Vegas LTD. The group also consisted of Garry Galloway on keyboards; Chris Wheatley, who we nicknamed "The Zooster," on bass; and a cute and talented newcomer, whom I had briefly dated years earlier, Kathy Lamb, on vocals. Later, we replaced Kathy with the sultry and sexy Barbara Sauter. My good buddy Tim Rice at Gail & Rice talent agency got us several great bookings including a two-month engagement at the luxurious D B's supper club located inside the newly constructed Hyatt Regency Dearborn, where we opened for such national acts as The Association, Glenn Yarbrough, and stand-up legend, Norm Crosby.

On March 24, 1976, Kenneth Jay Mills II was born at 9:31 a.m. at Botsford General Hospital. We were relieved that Connie's delivery proceeded without any complications and overjoyed because we were really hoping for a boy. It was an awesome day—a day I'll never forget for sure. I asked Sonny to be godfather to baby Kenny. He agreed, and our bond grew even tighter. I thought it was very cool that my first child was a "masculine child" and that he had an Italian godfather. Sadly, my grandmother Ruthie hadn't lived to see the birth of her first great-grandson.

I hadn't talked to Ted Nugent in a few years and decided to call him to see how things were going. No more than three minutes into our conversation he asked me to re-join his band. Evidently, he wasn't thrilled with his current drummer, Cliff Davies. I explained to him that, unlike before, I now had a wife and kid, and needed to maintain a suitable income. He assured me money wouldn't be a problem. So, I accepted his offer and for a third time, became Ted Nugent's drummer … or so I thought.

During our discussion, Ted told me he was about to leave on a six-week concert tour and asked if I could come to his rehearsal studio in Ann Arbor for an informal jam before he left town. He said that his record producer would be there, and he wanted him to hear me play. I wasn't familiar with Nugent's recent material, and because this had all come up so suddenly, I'd had no time to prepare. But I knew Ted had confidence in me and dug the way I played, so I didn't see this as a problem. Besides, there would be ample time to learn his current set list while he was out on the road.

The following afternoon when I arrived at the studio, one of Nugent's co-record producers, either Tom Werman or Lew Futterman was there, leaning against a wall. I believe it was Tom Werman, though he didn't introduce himself or shake my hand. While I was setting up, Ted and his wife,

Sandy came over to chat. Nugent told me that he was excited about a new song he'd written called "Cat Scratch Fever," and thought it had the potential to be a big commercial hit. Ted said that Sandy had come up with the title, and then in his own inimitable style, he choked out a few bars of the song. For some reason, vocalist and rhythm guitarist, Derek St Holmes, wasn't there that day, so I, Ted, and bassist, Rob Grange jammed for about an hour or so. During the jam session, Ted ripped through a few tunes from his latest LP. Since I didn't know the arrangements, some of the songs came out quite rough.

Either that night or the next day, I got a call from Ted. He said that although he really wanted me in his band, his record producer hadn't been impressed with me, and had talked him into keeping Davies. I didn't believe what I was hearing, as I knew full well from past experience that Nugent always had the final word on all decisions regarding his band personnel. I felt as though Ted had duped me. Afterwards though, the thought occurred to me that, similar to my Seger audition, perhaps being unprepared had once again bitten me in the ass and cost me a position in a band. I later learned that Cliff Davies had originally been brought in by Werman and Futterman to co-produce Ted Nugent's 1975 self-titled album, and that he eventually took over as drummer for Ted's group. So naturally these producers, who were tight with Davies, were going to advise Nugent against replacing him with me.

Rusty Day, having left his band, Cactus, was back in Michigan and living in a two-story brick and stone house just outside of Southfield, a northern suburb of Detroit. He was now fronting the band, Detroit, an offshoot of The Detroit Wheels formed by band member and drummer,

Johnny "Bee" Badanjek. Rusty had moved on from Marcia and was now seeing Sharon, a skilled equestrian from an affluent family.

Rusty was still very much involved in drugs and had become one of the area's biggest dealers. He was known for the high quality of his products and was widely acknowledged as a connoisseur by his peers. I was always welcome at Rusty's home and could come over anytime, "day or night," a privilege I didn't take lightly or abuse. He was ever the gracious host who kept aside stashes from previous buys to entertain friends who dropped by. It wasn't uncommon for me to be offered a line of pure Peruvian flake cocaine or a joint of high-grade marijuana.

One dark and gloomy day, I heard dark and gloomy news on the street that a shooting had taken place at Rusty's house. Word was that Rusty had shot Sharon with a handgun, leaving her paralyzed from the waist down. I didn't believe it, so I rushed over to Rusty's to see if it was true. It was. Rusty was at the house when I got there and told me that the whole thing had been a tragic accident, and that Sharon had agreed not to press charges against him. Nevertheless, he was feeling the heat from the local police and believed he needed to get out of town. Soon after, I heard that Rusty and Sharon quietly moved to Central Florida.

Sonny Cingolani was happily married and had an undying love for his wife and children. Even so, he often indulged his unrelenting lust for attractive women. Therefore, it wasn't surprising that soon after Barbara Sauter joined our Las Vegas LTD band, Sonny began an affair with her. At that time, I was also behaving in an adulterous manner, fooling around with a girl I had met at a bar called

The Pier 500 in Wyandotte on the Detroit River, where our band often played.

Late one night, when I got home from a gig, Connie was waiting up, ready to blindside me. She nervously recounted that earlier in the evening, she had received a phone call from Nancy Cingolani, Sonny's wife. Nancy, suspicious that Sonny was stepping out on her, had hired a private investigator to have him followed. As the PI had snapped photos of Sonny and Barbara together at a motel, he had also gotten shots of me and my girlfriend there together.

It's hard to put into words how I felt at that moment. I was humiliated having been exposed as a cheat, but for some inexplicable reason, my fury with how my indiscretions had been uncovered dictated the impulse of my response. Infuriated, instead of apologizing to Connie for my unfaithfulness, I kicked her out. I told her that our marriage was over and that she was to take the baby and walk. Then I left and didn't come back for days.

Returning home from moping and aware of how much I had missed Connie and the baby, I discovered they were gone. Reality stabbed at my heart, and as I stood alone in the silent apartment, I was devastated at the effect my cruelty had had on my family. As I envisioned a future without them, I vowed that, no matter what it took, I would reunite my family.

A day or two later, Connie phoned to tell me she'd moved to Florida. Her parents had wired her money to fly down and live with them in Altamonte Springs, a suburb of Orlando, where they had retired a couple years earlier. I expressed how truly sorry I was for my selfish and irresponsible behavior, and how I didn't want to give up on our marriage. She told me she didn't want to give up on our marriage either. So, we agreed to stay together and to make a fresh start by me moving to Florida to join her and little Kenny. Considering that we had no funds to finance this plan, I knew it wouldn't be easy.

I thought about people I knew in Florida who might be able to help me. Concert promoter/band manager, Mike Jezowski, still living in West Palm Beach, came to mind. Mike was Ted Nugent's brother-in-law and a big fan of The Amboy Dukes. I knew he thought highly of me and my talents, even though six years earlier, I had wrecked his brand-new Cutlass skidding into a telephone pole in Miami. I contacted Mike to explain my plan and see if he had any suggestions for me. Mike proposed that if I moved to West Palm, he could put a band together around me and manage my career with the goal of landing a record deal. Astonishingly, he also threw in a salary and a place to live. JACKPOT!!!! This was the perfect solution! I practically jumped through the phone with excitement as I gleefully accepted the offer.

On the first day of fall in 1976, I once again said my goodbyes to Sonny and my dad and Detroit, then loaded my drums and a few other items into my beat-up Dodge Dart (which, incidentally, was flagged for repo), and headed south on I-75 toward the Sunshine State. On the way to West Palm, I stopped in Altamonte Springs and spent a night with my wife at a Days Inn. There, we reaffirmed our love for each other. When it was time for me to hit the road the next morning, I assured Connie that I would send for her and the baby as soon as I got established in West Palm Beach.

Chapter Fifteen: The Pelicans

$\mathcal{I}$ hit West Palm at high noon and met with Mike Jezowski at an old rundown pub his family owned and operated, Hot Nights in the South, located near the heart of the city on Okeechobee Boulevard. When I walked in, Jezowski greeted me with a hearty hug. Then he stuck an umbrella cocktail in my hand, stuffed some cash in my pocket, and took me into his office to talk. I told him that I thought we should form an all original, high energy rock band in the image of The Amboy Dukes; Jezowski liked the concept. I added that I was tired of sitting behind drums staring at bandmates' asses and that I now wanted to front a band and write the songs. He was all for that as well and enthusiastically said, "Let's do it!" To celebrate our alliance, we raised our glasses in a toast to our future success.

Hot Nights was open seven days a week from 11:00 a.m. to 2:00 a.m. By day, the bar, managed by Jezowski and his brother Andy, served as a haunt for a handful of regular town drunks. But at night, it transformed into a young-adult nightclub featuring a steady showing of the finest local and regional rock acts. Among the occasional bookings was Mike Pinera, a Miami-based celebrity guitarist whom

I vaguely knew from past encounters, and remarkably, The Pelicans, the newly-formed band of my longtime friend and mentor Rusty Day, who had taken off to Florida after accidentally shooting and paralyzing his girlfriend.

Jezowski had some other obligations to deal with before he could turn his attention to our project and help me find somewhere to live. So, for the time being, he offered to let me stay at his place. Later that day, I followed him home and got unpacked and settled in. That evening, I met his wife, Julie, and although she was cordial, I sensed that she wasn't pleased with these new living arrangements.

For the next couple of weeks, my daily routine comprised of watching morning cartoons, attending matinees at the Palm Beach Jai-Alai Fronton, and partying 'til closing at Hot Nights in the South. After about a month of this hedonism, Jezowski broke it to me one day that Julie was missing her privacy and wanted me out of the house as soon as possible. Shockingly, he added that he was going to need another four or five months to put our music concept in place. I sat there baffled, wondering what to do. I had come to Florida to find a job so I could be with my family, but now that reunion appeared unlikely to happen anytime soon.

As I pondered my options, it occurred to me to give Rusty a call to see what he had going on. To my amazement he told me that he, Sharon, and the members of his band, The Pelicans, all of whom were from the Motor City, were living together in Apopka, a little town adjacent to Altamonte Springs where Connie was staying. The Pelicans consisted of Rusty on lead vocals and blues harp, John Sauter on bass, Steve Dansby on lead guitar, Jody Blair on rhythm guitar, and Frankie Robbins on drums. Several online articles quote rock experts as saying that The Pelicans was a reincarnation of Rusty's former rock and blues band, Cactus. Although the band covered some Cactus arrangements such as "Evil," "You Can't Judge A Book By The Cover," and "Bro. Bill," as far as I know, they always played under the name The Pelicans.

I explained my situation to Rusty, and incredibly, he told me that his drummer, Frankie Robbins, had just quit and moved back to Michigan. He offered to let me fill in on drums and stay at his house until Jezowski was ready for me to return to West Palm. I gratefully accepted, knowing this would be an ideal way of resolving my immediate financial needs, as well as allowing me to be close by to my wife and son. The following day, I updated Jezowski with my plans. Then without knowing for sure if I'd be back, I drove to Apopka and moved in with Rusty and company. The bedrooms were taken, so I slept on the floor in a corner of the den.

Living in the house with Rusty and Sharon, the band members and I saw first-hand the arduous care Rusty had to give Sharon due to her paralyzed condition. He had to toilet her, bathe her, dress her, and assist her in and out of the wheelchair-accessible van he'd had to purchase. I can't imagine the level of helplessness and despair Sharon must have felt. Yet despite it all, she always managed to maintain a positive and upbeat attitude.

Rusty was the proud owner of a Rhodesian ridgeback named Pluto, and one fine Sunday afternoon, he brought the dog to the Sanford-Orlando Kennel Club on a family fun day and entered him in a racing event open to dogs of all breeds and sizes. In each of several contests, eight dogs were placed in starting boxes for a fifty-yard race. When Pluto's race went off, he stumbled out of the box and began running around in circles chasing his tail. The entire band and Sharon cheered and rooted from the stands, while Rusty, standing on the tiny dirt track among the other dog owners looking wildly out of place with his shoulder-length hair and long wizard-like beard, waved and coaxed his pet to the finish line. Good ol' Pluto never did complete the race; nevertheless, a good time was had by all.

My few months in Apopka were a bittersweet and frustrating time for Connie and me and our relationship. I wasn't welcome at her parents' house, and at Rusty's crowded home, there was no privacy for us at all. The meager amount of cash I made from playing in the band was barely enough to cover my room and board, and Connie, who was working part-time at Sears at the Altamonte Mall, earned next to nothing. We had no money to do anything and no place to be together as a family. So even though we were only a ten-minute drive from one another, it felt as though we were a million miles apart.

John Sauter, whom I'd gotten to know and like, played a unique and energetic lead-style of bass, and man let me tell you, he was one helluva great musician. I knew that if I could get him involved in my forthcoming enterprise with Jezowski, he would be a valuable asset. About four months after joining The Pelicans, at the very real risk of alienating myself from Rusty, I told Sauter what I had waiting for me in West Palm and asked if he might be interested in signing on. He enthusiastically accepted. I phoned Jezowski and told him that I had recruited the perfect bass player for our project. He was excited and said the time was right for me and Sauter to come to West Palm to get things started.

About a week or so later, Jezowski called back and said he had found temporary living accommodations for

Sauter and me at a vacant studio apartment in nearby Palm Beach Gardens, and that we should head down right away. I explained the arrangement to Connie and promised her once again, for the umpteenth time, that we'd be back living together before long.

When I told Rusty I was leaving and taking Sauter with me, I thought he might go crazy and kick my ass or something. After all, he had spent a lot of time and capital putting The Pelicans together, and with my and Sauter's departure, it would likely take months to find worthy replacements to get his band up and playing again. Surprisingly though, Rusty pretty much took it in stride, and no punches were thrown.

Chapter Sixteen: The Bad Boys

$\mathcal{M}$ike Jezowski informed Sauter and me that he had engaged the services of rock and roll journeyman guitarist, Mike Pinera, and two of his Son of Cactus bandmates, keyboardist Duane Hitchings and drummer Donny Vosburgh, for our newly-forming band. I had first met Pinera, formerly of Blues Image ("Ride Captain Ride") and Iron Butterfly ("In-A-Gadda-Da-Vida"), in 1970 when The Amboy Dukes shared a stage at a Miami concert with his band, Ramatam. (Ramatam featured Mitch Mitchell, the legendary and pioneering drummer best known for his work with the Jimi Hendrix Experience, and groundbreaking female guitarist April Lawton.) Jezowski had also hired us a roadie, his trusted friend, Louie Ballone.

Jezowski approached me with the idea of bringing his brother, Andy Jezowski (aka Andy James), into the band to share and trade off vocal duties with me. Andy had sung lead on Ted Nugent's *Call of the Wild* album and had a strong set of pipes. However, his voice had a certain operatic quality attached to it which seemed better suited for Broadway than rock music. What's more, he had the non-rock-like appearance of a John Davidson celebrity look-alike:

pretty boy next door. Although he didn't have the voice or the look for the hard-hitting, high-energy rock group I envisioned, I felt I owed it to Mike to let his brother in the band. So without voicing an objection, I told him that it would be fine with me.

Because Pinera, Hitchings, and Vosburgh were living in Miami at the time, Mike got us a warehouse for band practice in Pompano Beach, about halfway between Miami and West Palm Beach. He also paid each member of the group a weekly salary of $300, provided us with a state-of-the-art PA system, and as time progressed, gave us anything and everything we needed or wanted. I decided to name the band "The Last Laugh," but a month later, I changed it to "The Bad Boys." The group's first meeting and rehearsal was scheduled to take place at the warehouse.

Mike Pinera and his sidekicks arrived an hour fashionably late that day, eliciting a grand entrance as they sashayed in. Pinera, who had gained an enormous amount of weight since last I'd last seen him, was draped in a full-length, tent-like, pastel purple robe. As he approached me, I caught sight of white powder on his nose. Although this wasn't a problem for me (who am I to judge, right?), I thought it was weird that he didn't bother to even wipe it off, considering this was our first gathering. Following Pinera were a pint-sized, roly-poly character clothed in a karate gi of sky-blue velvet, and a rangy, fair-haired dude decked out in a dashing, custom-made gold brocade Nehru jacket. I was soon to learn that roly-poly was Donny Vosburgh, and snazzy-dresser was Duane Hitchings. They certainly didn't look like rock stars, but what they lacked in appearance, they made up for in musical ability. Disappointingly though, by the end of practice it seemed to me that, based on their overblown egos and overall lack of enthusiasm, these three hired guns had joined the band for no reason other than to collect a paycheck.

Within the next week or so, all the band members began relocating to the West Palm area, except for Pinera, who elected to remain in Miami. Jezowski gave me the money to move Connie and Kenny down, and for that, I remain eternally grateful. Connie and I rented a fully-furnished mobile home in nearby Lantana, and at last, we were a family again. John Sauter moved to Greenacres, located in the same area, with a girl named Denny, whom he had met at Hot Nights in the South. Both Hitchings and Vosburgh chose to reside in the town of Palm Beach, right across the bridge from downtown West Palm Beach.

With just a few rehearsals under our belts, we went into SRS International Recording Studios in Fort Lauderdale and cut four tracks: "(I Want) Love And Affection (Not The House Of Correction)," by Nathanial Mayer; "Sweet Rockin' Music," a take-off of the soul classic, "Sweet Soul Music," by Arthur Conley; "Breaking Point," an original song written by Sauter and me; and "Do What You Wanna Do," written and sung by Pinera. Bizarrely, after this session for reasons I can't recollect, we never saw or heard from Mike Pinera again.

As a replacement for Pinera, I immediately thought of Mike Nardone with whom I had briefly played at the tail end of my stint with The Fallen Angels in 1973. He was a creative guitarist, fluent in all contemporary styles. In addition, and of equal importance, he was reliable and trustworthy, not just another hired gun. I ran his background by Jezowski and got his approval to bring him onboard. Then phoning Nardone in Los Angeles where he was living at that time, I offered him a position in the group. He accepted and became the band's new guitar player.

When Nardone arrived, he rented an apartment on Singer Island, a few miles north of West Palm Beach, and as soon as he was settled in, we went straight to work. Within a week, Nardone and I co-wrote what I believe to be two of the band's best songs, "Requiem For A Rock 'N' Roll Star" and "Something You Said." "Requiem" was a dark piece about the dying career of a rock legend from a different world in a different dimension. "Something You Said" was a mellow love song I'd written for Connie.

We went back into SRS Studios and recorded these two songs. Andy and I traded off verses on "Requiem." Andy sang solo on "Something You Said," and man, I'll tell you what, he effin' nailed it! The song was ideal for his type of voice. Over the following weeks, Nardone and I co-wrote four other numbers, "Paid Killer," "House Of Pleasure," "In My Mind's Eye" and "Turn Up Your Radio." Regrettably, none of these tunes were ever studio-recorded.

I also co-wrote six songs with Duane Hitchings: "Paying For Protection," "Evicted," "Rookie Of The Year," "Dollar Sign Eyes," "Military School," and "Colombian." Jezowski got us a booking at Bayshore Recording Studio in Miami's Coconut Grove and within three days we recorded all six tunes. Eric Shilling, who later worked with superstars Gloria Estefan and Janet Jackson, did a masterful job producing, engineering, and mixing our recordings.

"Paying For Protection," "Evicted," "Rookie Of The Year," and "Dollar Sign Eyes" were songs loaded with energy and attitude, and in my opinion, were nothing short of rock and roll masterpieces. I sang lead on "Military School," a song of which I was particularly fond, and which begged the question: "Where are the girls in military school?" This was a raw and brash piece of music that had all the subtlety of an elephant's prick. In contrast, "Colombian," glorifying the exceptional marijuana to be had in Miami, featured a Calypso groove with a half-time feel. Hitchings played it with the steel-drum setting on his keys, and Andy sang it with a Jamaican accent. I always thought this number had commercial potential. I give you...

"Colombian"

If you like to smoke Colombian,
Miami is the place to come, Mon.
Gold is about three hundred a pound,
they say there's plenty to go around.

Ohhhh Colombian,
Gold Colombian.
The people come and they drive it away,
and keep an eye out for the D.E.A.

The Bon Ami tonight it sails,
It's said to carry three thousand bails.
And over the channel in a dark lagoon,
they unload the previous cargo by the light of the moon.

Ohhhh Colombian,
Gold Colombian.
The people come and they drive it away,
and keep an eye out for the D.E.A.

So, if your hometown is dry,
and sticks and stems don't make it no more.
Head on down try the weed you'll see,
Miami is the place for high society.

Ohhhh Colombian,
Gold Colombian.
The people come and they drive it away,
and keep an eye out for the D. E. A.

A few weeks after our recording session in Coconut Grove, we scored a great gig. Foreigner was scheduled to open for Ted Nugent at the Hollywood (Florida) Sportatorium, but a week before the concert, their guitar player, Mick Jones, broke his arm, forcing them to cancel. Somehow, Mike Jezowski was able to arrange for us, The Bad Boys, to take their place.

For our performance, Jezowski's mother, Edith, custom-designed a stage costume for me: a navy-blue satin suit with red rhinestone-studded arrows featured prominently on the pants legs and jacket arms. The night of the show, Sauter's girlfriend, Denny, painted a red arrow down the middle of my face, extending from my brow, down my nose, and to my chin, to match the outfit. Andy, Sauter, Nardone, and Hitchings sported their best rock and roll attire, and Vosburgh wore a colorful Karate gi. Vosburgh was always wearing those fakakta gis. I don't even think he knew Karate. It's *my* gut he wore those loose-fitting gis to hide *his* gut.

Hitchings had been bugging Jezowski to get him a Polymoog Synthesizer. Jezowski finally bought one, presenting it to Hitchings for the first time at our Sportatorium sound check. Hitchings eagerly took it out of the box and set it up onstage. As Nugent's opening act, we played a forty-five-minute set and closed with "Dollar Sign Eyes." At the end of that song, Jezowski handed me a stack of one-dollar bills, and I showered the crowd with money. I believe today they call that "Makin' It Rain!" We exited the stage to a standing ovation and returned for an encore. During our show, Nugent was onstage watching from behind the amps, and afterwards, made it a point to compliment me on my performance. Coming from him that meant a lot.

We had taped our performance on a reel-to-reel recorder, and a few days after the concert, Jezowski and I sat down and gave it a listen. To our shock and dismay we realized that Hitchings had been playing the Polymoog completely out of tune the entire set!! It was an embarrassingly bad dissonance of noise. I don't know what went wrong, but my guess is that Hitchings must have inadvertently rotated the variable pitch knob, causing the keyboard to be about a quarter-tone from standard pitch. He was probably unable to hear himself or to hear the guitars. Jezowski and I were so pissed, we decided we had to replace him. But not to worry—Hitchings landed on his feet, and later enjoyed great success co-writing and playing on four of Rod Stewart's biggest hits, "Da Ya Think I'm Sexy," "Young Turks," "Infatuation" and "Crazy 'Bout Her."

On my recommendation, we brought in my friend and gambling buddy, John Coury (aka John Corey), to take Hitchings' place. Coury and I had met a few years earlier on the Detroit music scene, instantly forming a bond as we found that we not only shared a passion for music, but for sports betting as well. Coury was a seasoned guitarist and pianist. He had previously played in a popular Detroit-based band called Sky with Doug Fieger; Fieger later became the founder and frontman of the Knack, best known for their worldwide hit, "My Sharona." With Sauter, Nardone, and Coury, our band now consisted of some of the best musicians Detroit had to offer.

Jezowski rented a large four-bedroom house where the band could live and practice. It was secluded on a 20-acre lot located on Military Trail, north of West Palm Beach. Coury moved in when he arrived and a short while later, Sauter moved in as did Andy and our roadie, Louie. We transformed the spacious living area into a practice room, and yeah, we even got ourselves a pool table.

Chapter Seventeen: Trouble

It was August of 1977 and Ted Nugent was flying high on the success of his hit single, "Cat Scratch Fever," which had reached #30 on The Billboard Hot 100 music chart. His popularity had soared and he was selling out arenas from coast to coast. Mike Jezowski mentioned to me that Ted and Sandy were in West Palm Beach for a day visiting with Edith and Chester Jezowski, so I decided to stop by to say hello. Not long after I got there, Ted, with Sandy at his side, sat me down and asked me to join his band as drummer again. This took me quite by surprise, as he was well aware of my ongoing project with his brothers-in-law. Without a second thought, I declined his offer and told him I felt I owed it to Mike and Andy, as well as the rest of the band, to stay with them and stick it out. In hindsight, although my decision would probably be labeled selfless and admirable, it may have been the biggest mistake of my career.

As a way to showcase The Bad Boys, Jezowski decided to put together a monster rock and roll concert at the Hollywood Sportatorium and include our band among the acts. I had recently found out that a Detroit-based band had already taken the name The Bad Boys, so I changed our band name to Trouble, and we performed at the concert under that name. The event was held on August 28, 1977, and was billed as "The Last Rock and Roll Concert of the Summer." The twelve-hour long show was emceed by the gravelly-voiced Wolfman Jack and featured performers Elvin Bishop, The Nitty Gritty Dirt Band, Roy Buchanan, Steppenwolf, Quicksilver Messenger Service, Jan Hammer, and Travis Moon.

Coury knew a successful English record producer named Chris Kimsey whom he had met at Olympic Studios in London when his former band, Sky, recorded their first album with legendary Rolling Stones producer, Jimmy Miller. Kimsey was tops in his field and had co-produced and engineered such hit albums as The Rolling Stones' *Sticky Fingers* and Peter Frampton's *Frampton Comes Alive!* Coury convinced Kimsey to come and see us at the concert, and Jezowski paid for his airfare and related expenses. Jezowski also invited several local record producers and concert promoters, so there was a lot riding on our performance.

I did a radio interview with Tom Webb on WSHE-FM (Fort Lauderdale-Miami) promoting Trouble and the upcoming event. I still have a cassette copy of it. Several times during the interview, I referred to myself and my fellow band members as swine and savages, and when the interviewer asked me, "What happens onstage with this band?" I replied, "I perform with a painted face to disguise my identity. I do this so when I'm offstage, people don't try to beat me!"

Because of Jezowski's pull as promoter, Trouble was scheduled to go on at 8 p.m., the perfect time at a concert like this. During our hour-long set and encore, I pulled out all the stops and in the middle of our opening number,

"Military School," I cannonballed off the stage and freak-danced in the aisles like a rabid animal. Throughout the show, I was conscious that I had to deliver an exceptional performance, but it appears I went too far. When reviews of our show came out, the Miami Herald wrote, "Trouble shows great promise, but they need to put a leash on their mad dog;" the mad dog being me. Disappointingly, although a few of the local record producers showed some interest in us and asked for demos, the one we most wanted to impress, Chris Kimsey, politely passed on the band. That, however, turned out to be the least of our worries.

The real problem was that the concert had been a complete and utter flop at the box office, causing Jezowski to lose a staggering amount of money. In retrospect, the likely cause of the low attendance was the fact that the event had been held the day before the new school year was to begin. Not long after counting the gate, Jezowski called the band together and said that he could no longer afford to pay us or to provide the band with housing. Once the paychecks stopped, Vosburgh promptly bolted from the group.

I met with Jezowski privately, and we agreed that given all he had invested, it was worth taking one last shot at a record deal. We felt that if we could get a notable producer to record and produce our material, it could possibly lead to a contract offer. Jezowski set a meeting with Allan Blazek who had co-produced Elvin Bishop's hit single, "Fooled Around and Fell in Love," and co-engineered The Eagles' multi-platinum album, *Hotel California*. Blazek often worked with groups at Bayshore Recording Studio, where we'd previously recorded several of our Bad Boy tunes.

When we met, Jezowski and I let Blazek know we wanted to retain his services and had him listen to our demo to see if there was anything he liked. He expressed an interest in the two songs I had co-written with Nardone, "Requiem For A Rock 'N' Roll Star," and "Something You Said," and agreed to work with us. We settled on his fee and scheduled a recording session at Bayshore to take place two weeks later. Jezowski and I were ecstatic and couldn't wait to tell the rest of the band.

With Vosburgh no longer in the picture, we needed to find a drummer who could fill his shoes. I'm sure I could have done the session, but I hadn't played in months, and for a project of this importance, we needed someone who was on top of his game. On Nardone's recommendation, we flew in a drummer from LA named Eddie Rodriguez who had formerly played in the famous Latin band, El Chicano.

The recording session was a success; producer Allan Blazek, engineer Eric Shilling, and each member of the band delivered the best of their talent to this effort. Our songs sounded phenomenal. Jezowski and I sent cassette copies of the songs to several major record labels and to practically everyone we knew in the music industry. But to our frustration, we got no offers. Subsequently, Trouble crumbled and fell apart. Afterwards, I stayed on in West Palm Beach while the others left in search of alternate musical opportunities.

John Sauter landed a gig with Ted Nugent and played on his certified gold album, *Weekend Warriors*, which was released in 1978 and featured Nugent classics "Need You Bad" and "Name Your Poison." Mike Nardone moved back to his hometown of Pontiac, Michigan, where he formed an upscale and versatile musical group, Nouveauté, featuring Wendy Pooley Rogelle, with whom I had briefly played in Hammer in 1973. More than forty years later, Nouveauté is still together and performs at the finest venues in and around the greater Detroit area. John Coury went on to have a successful career playing in touring bands with Rod Stewart, Don Henley, the Eagles and The Who.

As for Donny Vosburgh, he eventually drifted to Los Angeles and joined Fortress, a band that had just scored a record deal with Atlantic Records. Without consulting me, they recorded a rendition of "Requiem For A Rock 'N' Roll Star" for their upcoming album and titled it simply "Requiem." Fortunately, however, having been ripped-off years earlier by Marcus Malone on my song "Kelly," I'd had the foresight to copyright "Requiem For A Rock 'N' Roll Star." Upon learning this, Fortress' management company, Rubicon Music contacted me to work out a songwriter's agreement. I handed off negotiations to Mike Nardone who had co-written the song with me. Nardone struck a deal with their representative, Teri Piro, which resulted in the four members of Fortress receiving partial songwriter's credits for the song and netted Nardone and me advance-against-writer's royalties of $500 each. In 1981, Fortress released their album, *Hands In The Till*. The final number is "Requiem." On the record's center-label, the listed songwriters are Turner, West, Vosburgh, Souza, Mills, and Nardone. Cynically, I'm not surprised that since the initial advance, I've never received a cent in royalties.

Prior to launching Trouble I had promised Connie that if the band didn't make it, I'd quit music for good and get a "real job." True to my word, when Trouble fell apart, I did exactly that. Over the next few months, Connie and I had a rough go of it, but with the assistance of food stamps and some financial support from Connie's sister and brother-in-law, we managed to tough it out until we each found suitable employment. I took a position as a bill collector with a collection agency called Southern Credit Clearing, and Connie found a job as an accounts receivable clerk with National Linen.

One day, a short time after joining the straight world, I took my son Kenny to an afternoon birthday party for Ted Nugent's daughter, Sasha, at Mr. and Mrs. Jezowski's house. Ted was at the party and at some point, we stepped outside for a moment to have a quick talk. During our conversation, I mentioned to him that I had quit playing music and was working at a collection agency. Hearing this, he frowned in disappointment. Then, reaching into his shoulder bag, he pulled out his address book and a pen and, as I stood before him, crossed off my name, address, and phone number. My association with Ted Nugent had given me an identity and a high level of respect on the Detroit rock scene, and with a stroke of a pen, I was irrelevant and forgotten.

Chapter Eighteen:
The Murder of Rusty Day

$\mathcal{F}$ollowing my transition from Rock Star to Desk Jockey, I fell out of touch with most of my friends in the music business, but I did stay in contact with my old compadre, Rusty Day. He and Sharon were still living in Central Florida and had moved from Apopka to 173 Parsons Road, a secluded property near the bedroom community of Longwood. Rusty had gradually become less involved in music and more involved in dealing drugs on a full-time basis. We would talk on the phone about once a month and every now and then, he would surprise me by mailing me a no-return-addressed envelope containing cocaine. When Connie and I would come up from West Palm Beach to Altamonte Springs every couple of years to visit her parents, I always made sure to look him up and spend time with him, but only by myself—never with Connie, as she had no interest in Rusty whatsoever. We would meet at his house, drink suds, do lines, and then usually go hit the local strip clubs. Rusty seemed to know most of the strippers and would discreetly feed them coke for lap dances and who knows what else.

Sometimes though, we would do the complete opposite, getting in touch with our softer sides through checking out the surrounding area's more wholesome attractions such as the Wekiva Springs State Park or the annual Zellwood Corn Festival. Once, we actually went to a public tennis court and hit the ball around for a while, but we were laughably terrible and probably looked like two monkeys trying to fuck a football!

The last time I saw Rusty was over the Memorial Day weekend of 1982, four days prior to his murder. (The Dead Rock Stars Club website, as well as other similar sites, incorrectly lists his death date as March 6, 1982, though he actually died on June 3, 1982.) As the eighties kicked off, Rusty's ever-increasing consumption of cocaine was beginning to manifest its physical toll. He wasn't taking care of himself and had become gaunt and pale. He even spent the final year of his life hobbling around on a broken leg because he refused to go to a doctor to have it set.

For the holiday weekend, Connie and I had driven to Altamonte Springs to stay with her parents. On one of those evenings, around nine or ten at night, I dropped by Rusty's house without calling ahead as I had often done in the past. Rusty opened the door with a pistol in his hand. He asked me to raise my arms and proceeded to frisk me. I thought he was just messing around and laughed it off. In retrospect, I believe Rusty knew someone was gunning for him.

Rusty had a houseguest staying with him, a drug dealer from Detroit named Garth McRae. Rusty's 12-year-old son, Jocko, whose mother had sent him to live with Rusty on a permanent basis earlier that year, was home that night too. Sharon was out of town spending time with relatives up north. After Rusty tucked Jocko into bed for the night, he emptied a large bag of coke onto the coffee table and once we were all wasted, he handed Garth and me each loaded revolvers. As the three of us sat there armed, my trippy high had me feeling like I was a member of the Wild West's Hole-in-the-Wall gang.

Later in the evening, perhaps around midnight, we were in the middle of a deep but sincere cocaine-induced conversation, when suddenly we heard a noise from outside. With a frightened look, Rusty put his finger to his lips and whispered, "Shhhh." We sat still and silent, our guns raised and pointed at the door and our eyes and ears alert for anything that moved. After several scary minutes of nothing happening, we relaxed and soon resumed our rap session.

It was getting late and just as I was about to leave, Rusty shamed me into staying longer than I had planned to by claiming half-jokingly, half-not-so-jokingly, that I had only come over for the cocaine. I didn't get out of there until five in the morning. When I got in, Connie was up waiting for me. In addition to being worried, she was pissed! I was still on shaky ground with her parents, and I certainly hadn't helped matters by staying out all night. Later that morning, we headed back to West Palm Beach, and it took me the entire ride home to get myself out of the doghouse with her.

On Monday, June 7th, I got the devastating news that Rusty, Jocko, and Garth had been the victims of a drug-related triple murder. In speaking to Sharon, reading about the shootings in the *Orlando Sentinel* newspaper, and from several other sources, these are the events surrounding Rusty's murder:

On the afternoon of Thursday, June 3rd, just days after I'd visited Rusty, an unnamed acquaintance of Rusty's entered the Parsons Road residence and found the bodies of Rusty and Jocko lying on the living room floor, the television still blaring. He came upon Garth's body in a bedroom. The acquaintance, who was not considered a suspect, called Seminole County Sheriff deputies to the scene, who determined the three had been dead for about 13 hours. They concluded that Rusty and Jocko had been forced to their knees and then executed with gunshots to their heads and chests. It was also known but never publicly released that Garth was discovered hiding in a closet, crouched in a defensive position, having been shot in the face through his raised hand. More than ten handgun shell casings were scattered through the house, but no murder weapon was recovered. Autopsies showed that each victim had been shot either three or four times. It haunts me to think that had my visit with Rusty been a few days later, I might have been murdered too.

Although investigators had no suspects, they were convinced that the person or persons responsible for the killings knew Rusty, as they found no sign of forced entry and nothing to indicate a struggle. They also ruled out robbery as a motive since $2,000 and an undetermined amount of cocaine remained in the house and other valuables, including many rifles and handguns, were not disturbed.

These murders are still unsolved. However, a few years ago, I came across the following entry in Wikipedia (not always to be trusted) whose contributor claimed to know exactly who killed Rusty and why:

"In 1982, Rusty Day was working on an album with Uncle Acid & the Permanent Damage Band, as well as dealing cocaine. Day owed money to Ron Sanders, one of the guitar players in his band, after a minor cocaine deal. Monte "Mondo" Thomas, Day's lead guitarist and close friend, explained Sanders as: "...a madman, he was a millionaire and a real bad coke fiend." Thomas and Day both lived in Day's house in Longwood, Florida, along with Day's 11-year-old son Russell [Jocko]. Thomas had agreed to drive a friend out of town and was therefore not present when Sanders opened fire with a machine gun, shooting through the windows in Day's house, killing Day, his son Russell, and a house guest, Garth McRae. Ron Sanders shot himself six weeks later after police had surrounded his house due to charges entirely different from the triple murder weeks before."

Through my own personal knowledge and research, the majority of this claim is a bunch of conjured up bullshit. Rusty, Jocko, and Garth were not killed by a machine gun fired through the windows. They were shot inside the house at close range. Also, I'm certain that this Monte Thomas individual never lived with Rusty and Sharon. Furthermore, Rusty had played in bands with some of the best musicians in rock and roll history. Knowing him as well as I did, I'm sure he would have mentioned it to me if he had been in a band called Uncle Acid & the Permanent Damage Band with Sanders and Thomas. And, knowing him as well as I did, I'm sure he never would have teamed up with these two losers.

Through newspaper articles in the Ocala Star-Banner and the Daytona Beach Morning Journal as well as other online sources, here's the dope I found on Rusty's suspected killer, Ron Sanders: Ronald L. Sanders was a self-employed building contractor, part-time amateur guitarist, and known large-scale cocaine dealer. He had an extensive record of drug arrests and convictions. He resided in a split-level home in an exclusive suburb in Volusia County, home of Daytona Beach. Law enforcers in Longwood's Seminole County had been aware of Sanders' dubious relationship with Rusty for some time and after "The Parsons Road Murders" took place, they desperately wanted to question him about Rusty's death. However, Sanders refused to talk to them.

In the late afternoon of Saturday November 6, 1982, the Volusia County Sheriff's Department received a report from one of Ron Sanders' neighbors of a gunshot from inside his house. Sanders was engaging in a verbal altercation with Janeen Barks, his girlfriend of two years and mother of his child. (Law enforcement officers on more than one occasion had been summoned to Sanders' home to quell his disputes with her.) The argument escalated out of control and in a rage, Sanders grabbed a handgun and shot Barks in the head, seriously injuring her.

Deputy Ernie Harris was sent to Sanders' house to check out the gunshot and domestic disturbance complaint. As Harris approached the residence, Sanders fired at him through a bedroom window, the bullet ripping through Harris' chest. Sanders then took Banks and their toddler, Heather, hostage for an hour or so before releasing them.

By then, police special-weapons teams and emergency vehicles had surrounded the house, and authorities were trying to convince Sanders to surrender. He answered at times with gunfire. Deputy Steve Saboda was sent to approach the rear doors of the house and while he was looking for a vantage point in which to toss a tear-gas canister, Sanders fired a rifle blast at him, tearing through Saboda's lightweight bullet-proof vest and passing through his spleen and heart, killing him instantly.

Rather than surrender, Sanders ended his own life less than two hours later with a shot to his temple at near point-blank range. According to authorities, Sanders died with a .38 caliber revolver in his left hand, a Ruger mini-14 high-powered assault rifle in his right hand, and cocaine in his bloodstream.

Janeen Barks was treated at Florida Hospital in Orlando for a bullet wound to her scalp which left her arm partly paralyzed. Initial responder, Deputy Ernie Harris, was taken to West Volusia Memorial Hospital where he survived his chest wound.

At a press conference held two days after the incident, Volusia County Deputy Ed Carroll told reporters of a rumor that had Janeen Barks threatening to tell police what she knew about Sanders' connection to Rusty's death. Although Carroll mentioned the rumor, he wouldn't confirm it. Perhaps Ron Sanders was the deranged dog who gunned down Rusty; he certainly seemed capable of it. However, relying solely on the unsubstantiated Wikipedia article and deputy's rumor, I'm not 100% convinced he was the assailant.

Rusty's body was shipped to his beloved hometown of Garden City, Michigan for burial. He was cremated and his ashes are interred in a local cemetery. Rusty was revered by a great number of friends and fans. I'm sure they miss him as much as I do.

Though some might find this hard to believe, Rusty was a spiritual man and believed in Jesus Christ. Notably, he also looked much like how Jesus is depicted in many old paintings and films. I'm reminded of a comment about him that was neatly scribbled on the men's room stall at The Club Shangri-la around 1965 when my teenage-self first met him. It said, "Rusty Day, Son of Christ!"

Chapter Nineteen: Dad's Demise

$\mathcal{N}$ear the end of 1976, my father married his third wife, Sarah Oddo, the daughter of his best friend Joe, and with whom he'd had his (second) scandalous affair. They eventually moved from the Botsford Apartments in Farmington Hills to a nice single-family home they'd purchased in the suburbs of Southfield. Dad again reentered the world of collections and within a few years was able to accomplish the arduous task of obtaining a private investigator's license. Now legally qualified, he opened a private detective agency specializing in surveillance, asset investigations, and credit profiles. He named his business "Saradon Investigations."

To service his clients' requests for information, he relied heavily on the use of false-pretext phone calls to trick subjects into disclosing personal and confidential employment and financial details. My father was considered by his peers to be a pioneer and master of this unethical practice.

In the summer of 1980, my dad had a non-fatal, yet serious heart attack. Concerned, I decided to fly to Detroit for a weekend to see him, but about an hour before the plane was scheduled to take off, the strangest thing happened.

I was riding up the escalator at the Palm Beach International Airport, waving good-bye to Connie and Kenny. Just when I reached the top and stepped off, a thin blonde-haired girl with ghost-white skin and wide, piercing eyes moved toward me and called out, "Hey K J!" I didn't recognize her at first and stood there awkwardly, trying to decide how I should respond. As she got closer, she said, "Don't you recognize me? We used to live together!" She had a deep, sexy voice. And then it came to me. It was Wendy, the girlfriend who had so coldly dumped me almost ten years earlier. We discovered that we were on the same flight and when we boarded, the plane was nearly empty, so we were able to sit together for the entire trip.

She told me right away that she was still living in Ann Arbor with the same guy she'd left me for. Yet surprisingly, after a couple of cocktails, she started coming on to me. As we made our descent into Detroit Metro Airport, she handed me her number on a little a piece of paper and said temptingly, "My boyfriend is out of town for the next couple of days. Call me if you're free." After we parted ways in the terminal, I threw her number in the trash and immediately felt a satisfying sense of retribution.

When I got to the hospital, my old man told me his doctor had warned him that if he didn't stop overeating and continued to smoke, he was going to die. But food was my dad's reason for living. He had *dreams* about food, in Technicolor no less. And when it came to smoking, he'd been at it since he was a teenager, going through three to four packs of Kools a day. So for him, giving up a lifetime of these bad habits wasn't going to be easy.

Like my father, I, too, smoked heavily, more than two packs of Winstons a day. To encourage him to give up cigarettes, I made him a deal. I promised that if he stopped smoking, I would too. So we quit together, cold turkey, and implausibly, we were *both* successful in kicking the habit once and for all. My dad also managed, in just a matter of months, to drop thirty pounds. However, despite this accomplishment, within a year he managed to gain it all back and more.

My dad's business was beginning to boom, and he was raking in the dough. At the beginning of 1984, he and Sarah sold their home and bought a luxurious high-rise condo in metro Detroit's Southfield Town Center. They sure knew how to spend money, purchasing several new cars, including a jet-black Fleetwood Cadillac Brougham, and taking frequent vacations to the Caribbean. In short, they were "livin' large!"

Five years later, my father suffered a debilitating stroke which severely impaired his speech. While this would be a crisis for anyone, my dad depended on his voice for his livelihood. But, when I tell you what he did to conquer this challenge, I think you'll agree that it was nothing short of genius. When he got back to work following his stroke, he deceptively resumed his deceptive phone-calls, telling the subjects that he had just come to America from Germany and was still learning how to speak the English language. Though he could barely articulate a sentence, he was such a skilled bullshit artist that this ploy worked for him almost every time. Fortunately, after months of speech therapy, he fully regained his ability to talk.

In the mid 90's, Dad and Sarah divorced, but continued to live together off and on. Although the reason for their split is not entirely clear to me, I suppose it was most likely inevitable, due to their almost twenty-five-year age difference.

In autumn of 1996, my dad's health again took a bad turn. He was experiencing shortness of breath and his feet and ankles had swollen to an alarming size. Dad was admitted to the intensive care unit at the Detroit VA Medical Center. Doctors determined that his heart was only working at 25% of its capacity, so he was diagnosed with congestive heart failure. Connie and I drove to Detroit to visit him in the hospital. While we stood at his bedside, he told us, with a quivering voice and teary eyes, that he had been given less than six months to live. This was the only time in my life I ever saw my father cry.

After several weeks in intensive care, my dad was transferred to an assisted-care facility to live out his remaining days. About four months after being admitted, and against medical advice, he checked himself out. Sarah, now a live-in caregiver, had been hired by an elderly man in Dearborn to move into his home and attend to his needs. My dad moved in with them.

On the morning of March 2, 1997, Sarah called to tell me that my dad had suffered a massive heart attack and had been rushed to Oakwood Hospital in Dearborn. Later that day, I received a phone call from a hospital social worker who informed me that my father was brain dead. She asked for my permission to disconnect his life-support system. Knowing my dad's wishes, I gave my authorization to do so. The hospital faxed some paperwork to me; I signed my father's life away and faxed it back. Within an hour, the hospital called again to tell me that my dad had passed away.

His body was cremated and his ashes were buried at the Fort Custer National Cemetery in Augusta, Michigan in section E, site 570. None of my father's friends or surviving relatives has ever contacted me regarding his resting place. As I write this, no one who knew him has visited his grave.

About six months after my dad's death, Sarah called me to say that she had moved to Florida and was living in Daytona Beach. After that, I never heard from her again. In 2001, I learned that she had passed away in Volusia County about a year earlier in May of 2000. I made some inquiries, but was unable to find out her cause of death or place of burial.

Chapter Twenty:
Time Passes, Things Change

$\mathcal{I}$n the wake of the 80's housing boom, Connie and I bought our first house. It was a nice starter home in the suburbs of West Palm Beach. On February 10, 1982, our second son, Michael Scott Mills was born at 10:00 p.m. at Good Samaritan Hospital. Another boy! How great is that?! In March of 1983, we sold our home in West Palm and moved back to Central Florida, where we lived in Altamonte Springs, and more recently, Longwood, ever since. For many fun and proud years, I helped coach Kenny's and Michael's Altamonte Springs little league baseball teams. Both were terrific ballplayers and made their respective all-star teams every season.

I went to work as a bill collector for a collection agency called Creditors Mercantile located in the Koger Executive Center in Orlando. A few years later, I resigned and took a position as a collection supervisor for Payco (one of the country's largest debt-collection agencies) located in the Maitland Center Business Park in the Orlando suburb of Maitland. In March of 1989, I left Payco and started my own collection agency, Advance Recovery, specializing in conducting extensive asset investigations and skiptrace investigations for insurance companies and law firms. My company was just like my father's, except, unlike him, I ran my shop in a legal and ethical manner.

In 1997, at age 47, after twenty years away from music, I decided it was time to get back in the game again. I purchased a set of Roland electronic drums and a Fender amp and began practicing every chance I got. You know the old saying, "Once you learn how to ride a bike, you never forget." Well, when it came to drums, it didn't work that way for me. I found that I had forgotten even the *basics* of drumming, and I literally had to relearn how to play. Though my early influences were world-renowned drummers Clyde Stubblefield (James Brown), Mitch Mitchell (Jimi Hendrix), and Carmine Appice (Vanilla Fudge and Cactus), this time around, I drew my inspiration from super-talented up-and-coming drummers Mike Wengren (Disturbed), Scott Phillips (Creed), and Tommy Clufetos (Mitch Ryder, Ted Nugent, Alice Cooper, Rob Zombie, and the Prince of Darkness himself, Ozzy Osbourne).

My proficiency back after two years of woodshedding, I purchased a Pearl "Session Select" teal blue drum set and joined a local contemporary-rock band called "WRONG." The leader of the group, Bryan Smith, sang lead vocals and played keys. His younger brother, Mark Smith, a musically creative genius, played lead guitar. The other band members were Chad Lee on rhythm guitar, Dom Figueroa on bass, and moi on drums. These guys had waist-length hair and were half my age. They were a boisterous bunch and a blast to play and hang out with. I took the nickname, "Machine," inspired by a character in the cult-classic 1999 film, 8mm, and it stuck. We played creative, original songs with mile-a-minute tempos and were told we sounded like a cross between AC/DC and 90's rap metal band, Limp Bizkit. Some of our best numbers were "Wake Up Call," "Chic 'n' Head," "Pill Popper," "Phat Girl" and "Rug Burn." The band practiced in the backroom of Abyss, a head shop in nearby Fern Park. Pretty dope, eh?

WRONG had already been together for a few years before I joined and had built up a loyal following. We frequently performed at the Orlando locations of House of Blues and Hard Rock Live. We also played a lot at the FBI (Fairbanks Inn), Lost & Found, and the legendary Station in Fern Park.

Around that same time, Orlando-based comedian, Larry the Cable Guy, famous for his catch phrase, "Git-R-Done!" was making regular appearances on Central Florida radio shows. For one of his most memorable shticks, he organized the now infamous and intentionally un-PC, "Heterosexual Day Parade." On the day of the parade, about 50 decorated cars and trucks passed through the streets of Orlando, satirically celebrating "Straight Pride." Bringing up the rear was our band, playing on the back of a pick-up truck driven by a friend of the bands, the PA and amps powered by a generator. Roughly half-an-hour into the procession, our driver stopped too fast at a red light, throwing my ass down in the bed of the truck and burying me in my drum set. It was a cringe-worthy moment, but luckily, the only thing hurt was *my* pride.

Our greatest achievement was in 2001, playing the seventh annual Earthday Birthday concert in downtown Orlando. Hosted by Orlando radio's The Rock Station 101.1

WJRR, the show by now was regularly drawing 10,000 to 12,000 fans. In addition to our band that year, the 12-hour event featured Mudvayne, Tantric, Staind, and Disturbed.

In the latter part of 2001, we recorded a CD of original songs at Reel Time Studios, just north of Daytona in Ormond Beach. We named our CD *Bring It On.* For the front cover we used a picture of Bryan's three-year-old son locked inside a Pet Porter. (That's Just Wrong!) Once it was ready, we held a CD release party at Lost & Found and invited all our fans and friends to join us. In a touching move, my best friend, Sonny Cingolani, flew down from Detroit to attend the event.

Everything WRONG earned, which wasn't much, was used to cover the cost of our website, band merch and studio time. I truly dug playing with WRONG; however, I came from an era when musicians were able to earn a living playing in bands. So, soon after our CD was released, I made the decision to move on in search of a group where I could actually make money. The band subsequently broke up.

Twelve years later, I again joined WRONG when they decided to reunite. But not long after we began rehearsing, Bryan became mysteriously ill and was having difficulty singing, which nipped our reunion plans in the bud. We later learned that he had contracted stage 4 lung cancer which eventually spread to his brain. Tragically he passed away on February 14, 2015 at the age of 46, leaving behind his wife, Tricia, and three children. There will always be a place in my heart for my friend and bandmate, Bryan Smith.

In May of 2005, I dissolved my collection agency and became a full-time house-husband and part-time rocker. In June of 2008, as a former member of The Amboy Dukes,

I was honored to be inducted into the Michigan Rock and Roll Legends Hall of Fame. Other notable Michigan-based inductees have included Bob Seger and The Silver Bullet Band, Grand Funk Railroad, Mitch Ryder and The Detroit Wheels, Brownsville Station, Iggy Pop and The Stooges, and the Alice Cooper Group. On a side note: my old band, K J Knight and The Knightriders was nominated for the 2011 inductees.

On April 17, 2009, The Amboy Dukes were presented with a distinguished achievement award at the 18th annual Detroit Music Awards held at the Fillmore Detroit. In honor of the occasion, Nugent reunited the existing original and former members of The Amboy Dukes and played together with them for the first time in almost forty years. Sounds great, right? Except for one thing; I wasn't invited. That's right, I was snubbed.

The Amboy Dukes invited to perform that night were vocalist John Drake, bassist Bill White, rhythm guitarist Steve Farmer, and keyboardists Rick Lober and Andy Solomon. The Amboy Dukes' original drummer, Dave Palmer, whom I'd replaced when I joined the group, declined an invitation because, in Nugent's words, "He hadn't played in over thirty years and knew he wouldn't be able to catch up and get his chops together in such a short time." The next logical and rightful alternative for an Amboy Dukes drummer was me. But instead, Nugent brought in some guy who had never even been a member of The Amboy Dukes. His choice, Jimmy Butler, was a drummer who played in an early '60s Detroit-based band called The Gang. It felt like a slap in the face, but I guess in the grand scheme of things, it doesn't really matter that much. The Detroit Free Press wrote an article on April 15,

2009 about the ceremonies and award show and, from their news file archives, posted an old group photo of The Amboy Dukes. In what I consider to be poetic justice, the picture published with the article was of Nugent, Arama, Solomon, and yours truly.

On a starry night in late September of 2014, I joyfully discovered that I had a beautiful forty-four-year-old daughter named Starr Kuzak. You may recall that in 1970 while Ted Nugent and I were roommates, we had speculated briefly about the fatherhood of the baby of a pregnant girl we each had recently dated. When the baby was born, her mother had listed Nugent as the father on the birth certificate. As I mentioned earlier, I often wondered if the little girl was mine. All these years later, after genetic tests were done in the pursuit of knowledge for knowledge's sake, it was confirmed that I, not Ted, was Starr's biological father. Starr and I happily embarked on a life changing journey, a journey to the center of the heart! The DNA results established the probability of my paternity at 99.997%, with one possible mutation. (She and I like to joke that the mutation is her unusually long fingers.)

At first, I thought about what my role should be in Starr's life. She already had a good father in Nugent, who had brought her into his family when she was fifteen. I decided that being a supportive friend and cheerleader would be a good place to start. It is remarkable how quickly our bond has grown. We've become the best of comrades and are in constant contact with one another. We make each other laugh and tell each other we love one another at least once every day. I told Starr that when I was a little boy my parents had called me "Cowboy Kenny," so Starr decided she needed a make-believe name, too. We agreed she could be my Indian sidekick, "Rising Starr."

Not only do I now have a daughter whom I adore, through her I've also gained a son-in-law, granddaughter, and grandson. And check this out, just like grampa K J, my grandson plays the drums. How cool is that?! Starr is a devoted mom, supportive wife, and the best daughter ever. A Detroit resident, Starr is a staunch advocate of the city's revitalization. She's artistic in nature and passionate about literature and music (she plays violin!). Plus, she has a pet bearded dragon that she feeds by hand.

I flew to Detroit to be with Starr on her forty-fifth birthday. We had decided beforehand that we were going to jam together during my visit; we were super-stoked about it. Starr hadn't picked-up her violin in years, so to prepare, she had a professional restring her axe and spent hours honing her skills. On her birthday, with the accompaniment of my lifelong friend, guitarist Sonny Cingolani, my daughter and I knocked out a red-hot version of the classic bluegrass standard, "Blackberry Blossom." Starr hit it outta the park! I was tremendously proud of her. It was such a special father/daughter experience, a memory we will treasure forever. Starr named our group The Sun, Star, and Night Band, and posted a video of our performance on Facebook. (The band is currently open for bookings, LOL!) I love Starr with all my heart and soul. I'm so grateful to finally have her in my life.

In 2020, I hit the big 7-0, and I'm still kickin'. Unable to stay away from my passion for drumming and being part of a band, I currently play in a local, six-member classic rock group called Treble Damage (not to be mistaken for the Illinois band of the same that features former

Smashing Pumpkins' drummer, Matt Walker). My fellow bandmates are lead vocalist and percussionist Yvonne Belle, guitarist and vocalist Dan O'Brien, rhythm guitarist and vocalist Steve Ball, bassist and vocalist Dave Cannella, and keyboardist and vocalist Don Jensen. (Former band leader and lead vocalist, David Jones, sits in with us whenever he's in town.) We play upscale nightclubs, private parties, and various charity events.

Connie and I just celebrated our 46th wedding anniversary and are living our best lives together. Our sons, Kenny and Michael, have blessed us with a gaggle of amazing grandchildren who keep us young and on the move.

As for my criminal activities, I haven't stolen anything in over four-and-a-half decades, not even a pack of smokes. I seriously doubt I would ever go back to my old stealing ways, but I'm not making any promises. Who knows what tomorrow may bring?

SHOUT-OUTS

A big thanks to my inspirations and co-stars in life:

Garry Reese, Tomo, Howdy, Don Stoelt, Jeff White,
Jim Dasky, Stephanie "Stevie" Clark, Linda "Cricket" Brock,
Gary Beam, Steve "Muruga" Booker, Richard Shack,
Dale Peters, Jimmy Fox, Joe Walsh, Chip Fitzgerald,
Donnie Better, Gloria Peterson, Ron Silverman,
Brenda Stricklin, Marcia Day Hutchinson, Phil Nicholson,
Andy Solomon, Rob Grange, Danny Gore,
Dansir McCullough, Camelia Ortiz, Nancy Quatro Glass,
Skid and Carrie, Mitch Ryder, Bob Seger, Alice Cooper,
Iggy Pop, Scott Richardson, Robin Dale, Ray Goodman,
James McCallister, Jim McCarty, Johnny Bee Badanjek,
Wayne Kramer, John Sinclair, Scott Morgan,
Derek St Holmes, Jason Hartless, Tommy Clufetos,
Carmine Appice, Jack White, Dave Miller, Gloria Blondy,
Katie Doyle Elliott, Dawn Qualls Day, John Houghton,
Richard Koz Kosinski, Tim Rice, Marcella Detroit,
Shaun Murphy, Mike Nardone, Wendy Rogelle,
John Sarkisian, Jimmy Recca, Brett Sobering-Hattaway,
John Sauter, Steve Dansby, Pat Appleson,
Dmytro Doblevych, Steve Miller, Tom Wright,
Bruno Ceriotti, Kim Maki, Frank Pettis, Kim O'Steen,

Robert Klein, Pete Rose, Mark Kracht, Terri Kracht,
Steve Finly, Michael Finly, Don Sanderson, Mark Smith,
Julie Smith, Chad Lee, Dom Figueroa, Tricia Rine Smith,
Bryan Bonner, Robert Gillespie, Susan Hudak-Scherer,
Dee Gilbert, Wesley Dolen, Dave Defoe, Jeff Coda,
Pete Chinelli, Steve Ethridge, Janet JJ Schultz,
Marc Schwartz, Jill Schwartz, Richard Wright,
Lynnette McFadden Wright, Suzy Overall, Betsy Serafin,
Don Rogozinski, David Jones, Steve Ball,
Dawn Chiary Ball, Dan O'Brien, Terri Skelton,
Don Jensen, Yvonne Belle, Logan Belle, Dave Cannella,
Rebecca L. Palmer, Jay Yochem, Rich Nice, Rick Navarro,
Brittany Mills, Riley Joliet, Steve Bouman, John Bauder,
Chris Kuzak, Kat Petty, Kevin Lange, James Bauder,
Steve DeBoskey, Sabra Bateman, Jason Bateman,
Keri Patterson Nestle, Erik Nestle, Terry Valdez,
Ronald Walton, Debbie Modrak Gruszka, Bobby Lewis,
Bill Farmer, Freddy Bender, John Barnwell, Richard Fidge,
Nikki Corvette, Mary Cobra, Michael Anthony Smith,
Terry Whittenburg, Shelley Rigney, Jan Rugg-Sullivan,
Michael Krawczyk, Pete Castelli, Pete Jamestone,
Claudio Fabian Salimbeni, KC Jones, Mike Boggio III,
Beth Kephart, Jill Benner, Sasha Nugent, Chantal Nugent,
Ted Fleetwood Nugent, Danielle Nugent,
Louisa Elers Savarese, Heather Ballinger, Dan Murphy,
Rick Quest, Kevin Walters, Michael Edell,
Denise Mandell Hughes, Pat O'Hern, Randy Meyers,
Jeff Faust, Rick Lober, Linnea Arama Hamilton,
Dory Schmidt, Chris Foveros, Steve Hughey, Bill Soudrette,
Richard Brown, as well as the many others with whom I've
shared my journey.

MICHIGAN ROCK AND ROLL ROYALTY

The following home-bred bands have been inducted into the Michigan Rock and Roll Legends Hall of Fame:

The Rationals, an Ann Arbor-based band, featured lead vocalist and frontman, Scott Morgan, regarded as Michigan's most expressive rock singer of the mid-to-late '60s. Band members consisted of guitarist Steve Correll, drummer Bill Figg, and bassist Terry Trabandt. The group had several successful singles including a remake of Otis Redding's "Respect," which ended up reaching #92 on the Billboard Hot 100.

The Flaming Ember, a blue-eyed soul band, scored three pop and rhythm-and-blues hits in 1969-70 for Holland-Dozier-Holland label Hot Wax: "Mind, Body, and Soul," which reached #26 on Billboard pop-singles chart; "Westbound No. 9," which was a #24 hit on the pop chart and a #15 hit on the Billboard R&B chart; and "I'm Not My Brother's Keeper," which made it to #34 on the pop chart and #12 on the R&B chart. The original band members were guitarist Joe Sladich, keyboardist Bill Ellis, bassist Jim Bugnel, and lead vocalist and drummer, Jerry Plunk.

Rare Earth, a soul band eponymous with Motown's Rare Earth record label, had a number of Top 40 hits in 1970–71, including remakes of The Temptations' songs "(I Know) I'm Losing You" and "Get Ready." Their covers were actually more successful than The Temptations' original versions. "Get Ready" became Rare Earth's biggest hit, peaking at #4 on the US Billboard Hot 100 chart. It sold over one million copies and received a gold record awarded by the Recording Industry Association of America. The original band members included lead vocalist and drummer Pete Riviera, guitarist Rod Richards, keyboardist Kenny James, saxophonist and flutist Gil Bridge, and bassist and trombonist John Persh.

Wilson Mower Pursuit was among the most popular live bands in their native Detroit during the late 1960s, often playing the famed Grande Ballroom. Their sound encompassed a cross between Haight-Asbury psychedelic and Detroit revolutionary power rock. Frontwoman and vocalist extraordinaire, Shaun "Stoney" Murphy had her career launched with WMP. In 1971, Murphy was signed by Motown Records. In 1973, after a period of inactivity she left the record label to work with Bob Seger. She has continued to sing with Seger on studio session work and on all of his tours ever since. Over her career she has also sung, toured, and recorded with Meat Loaf, Eric Clapton, Herbie Hancock, Joe Walsh, Bruce Hornsby, the Moody Blues, Michael Bolton, and Little Feat.

Another Michigan favorite was Julia, fronted by guitarist and vocalist Blue Miller (aka Bill Mueller). The band released a handful of singles and opened for acts like Fleetwood Mac and The Lovin' Spoonful.

Third Power, a psychedelic hard rock power trio released one album, *Believe*, in 1970, which resulted in modest sales. The band's guitarist, Drew Abbott, is best known for playing in Bob Seger's Silver Bullet Band. In 1981, Abbott won a Grammy in the Best Rock Performance by a Duo or Group with Vocal category for his work on the Seger album, *Against the Wind*.

Frijid Pink was a rock band best known for their distorted guitar-driven rendition of "House Of The Rising Sun," which reached the Top Ten on US Billboard's Hot 100 in the spring of 1970 and sold more than one million copies. The original band members were lead vocalist Kelly Green, guitarist Gary Ray Thompson, bassist Tom Harris, and drummer Rick Stevers.

Teegarden & Van Winkle, featuring the musical duo of David Teegarden on drums and vocals and Skip (Knape) Van Winkle on electronic organ, organ pedal bass, and vocals, were best known for their 1970 smash "God, Love, And Rock & Roll (We Believe)."

Sunday Funnies was comprised of lead vocalist Richard Fidge, guitarist Ronald Aitken, drummer Richard Mitchell, and keyboardist Richard Koz Kosinski. After debuting in 1970 with a successful cover of Bob Seger's hit single, "Heavy Music" issued on the local Hideout label, the Sunday Funnies released its notable self-titled debut LP a year later on Motown's Rare Earth label.

The Jagged Edge, a heavy psych and acid rock band, were known for notorious, enigmatic frontman, Dave "Stoney" Mazar and their wild stage presence. The group had a strong local following and was a regular opening act at all the major Michigan rock and roll venues.

In 1967, guitarist and vocalist Glenn Frey, a native Michigander and a founding member of the Eagles, put together the Mushrooms with Jeff Burrows on keyboards, Bill Barnes and Doug Gunch on guitars, and Larry Mintz on drums. The band scored a major coup by having Bob Seger write both sides of their first single, "Such A Lovely Child" and "Burned." Seger produced the session as well. Glenn and the Mushrooms promoted their record twice while featured on Robin Seymour's Swingin' Time television show. Although the Mushrooms sole record didn't set the charts on fire, they were a regular and respected fixture on the local live scene.

The Up, considered by many as one of the forefathers of punk rock, consisted of lead vocalist Frank (Dedenbach) Bach, guitarist Bob Rasmussen, bassist Gary Rasmussen, and drummer Victor Peraino. The band was closely related to the MC5, as both bands' members lived in White Panther Party founder John Sinclair's commune. In May 1968, Sinclair moved the commune from Detroit to Ann Arbor and both bands followed. In 1970, The Up released a fan-favorite single pressed on red vinyl, "Just Like An Aborigine." One of the things I remember about this group is that they were all super-thin, which was rumored to be the result of rigid macrobiotic dieting. This, at the time, seemed bizarre to me.

In Memoriam

Luther Allison
John Angelos
Greg Arama
Ron Asheton
Cynthia Blondy
Jack Burningtree
Sonny Cingolani
Mike Collins
Pat Dougherty
Terry Dougherty
Russell "Jocko" Davidson Jr.
Rusty Day
Angel Diaz
Jon Finly
Verna Finly
Garry Galloway
Dave Gilbert
Slim Harpo
Sherman Hemsley
Gary Huntley
Lee Huntley

Andy Jezowski
Edith Jezowski
Mike Jezowski
Terry Kelly
Cubby Koda
James Lipton
Ray Manzarek
Richard Haddad Michaels
Don Mills
Ruthie Reinholtz Mills
Sarah Mills
Johnny Nugent
Sandra Nugent
Mike Opolski
Gary Quackenbush
Rob Ruzga
Bryan Smith
Rick Stewart
Larry Walton
Thomas Yochem
Al Zsenyuk

PROUST QUESTIONNAIRE

A note to my readers:

Perhaps you're familiar with the long-time acclaimed Bravo series, *Inside the Actors Studio*, hosted for 22 seasons by James Lipton, dean emeritus of the Actors Studio Drama School at Pace University. In each episode, Lipton interviews a notable actor in front of an audience of Actors Studio Drama School students, in order that they may learn a bit about the psyche of the featured guest.

For the interviews, Lipton asks his guests a set of ten questions inspired by French journalist, Bernard Pivot's adaptation of the Proust Questionnaire. The show is taped in a very formal and austere setting. Occasionally, an actor's quip will elicit some laughter, but for the most part, the mood is very solemn and dignified (although Eddie Murphy was once featured as a guest).

Of course, I'm sure you're now curious as to how I, a notable musician, would respond to these questions…

James Lipton: And now, *Inside the Actors Studio* presents notable musician, Mr. K J Knight.
Audience: (reserved applause)

Lipton: What is your favorite word?
K J: Fakakta

Lipton: What is your least favorite word?
K J: Queef

Lipton: What turns you on creatively, spiritually, or emotionally?
K J: Girls Gone Wild

Lipton: What turns you off?
K J: Bullshitters

Lipton: What is your favorite curse word?
K J: Motherfucker

Lipton: What sound or noise do you love?
K J: Applause

Lipton: What sound or noise do you hate?
K J: Gunshots

Lipton: What profession, other than your own, would you like to attempt?
K J: Professional Gambler

Lipton: What profession would you not like to do?
K J: Men's Room Attendant

Lipton: If Heaven exists, what would you like to hear God say when you arrive at the Pearly Gates?

K J: "Come on in! The drinks are on the house!"

Audience: (WILD STANDING OVATION!)

K J: (flourished actor's bow)

Printed in the United States
By Bookmasters